SECRETS
OF THE
SUPERNATURAL

SECRETS
OF THE
SUPERNATURAL

Investigating the World's Occult Mysteries

Joe Nickell
with John F. Fischer

PROMETHEUS BOOKS
Buffalo, New York

90   4 3

Library of Congress Cataloging-in-Publication Data

Nickell, Joe.
    Secrets of the supernatural.

    1. Supernatural—Case studies. I. Fischer, John F.
II. Title.
BF1029.N53   1988   133   88-12633
ISBN 0-87975-461-3

CONTENTS

ILLUSTRATIONS

FIGURES

TABLES

ACKNOWLEDGMENTS

We are most grateful to Paul Kurtz, publisher of Prometheus Books, for inviting us to compile this casebook and seeing it through to completion.

Thanks are also due the many persons and institutions who assisted in our investigations. In addition to those listed in the acknowledgments of the individual chapters, we would like to express our appreciation to Lieut. Drexel T. Neal, Lexington-Fayette Urban County Division of Police, Lexington, Kentucky, for special assistance; and to the dedicated staffs of the Margaret I. King Library, University of Kentucky, and the John F. Kennedy Memorial Library, West Liberty, Kentucky, for their help over the years.

We are also extremely grateful to Robert H. van Outer for continual photographic work, and to Ella T. Nickell for typing our investigative reports and articles and for subsequent help in preparing the manuscript for this book.

Finally, we appreciate the advice, encouragement, and repeated assistance of Jerome Clark, *Fate* magazine; Doris Doyle, Prometheus Books; and the staff of the Committee for the Scientific Investigation of Claims of the Paranormal—including Mark Plummer, Executive Director; Barry Karr, Public Relations Director; and Kendrick Frazier, editor of the Committee's journal, the *Skeptical Inquirer.*

1. INTRODUCTION
An Investigative Approach

The end is dark to me also, but I have hold of one idea which may lead us far.
                                        —SHERLOCK HOLMES
                        "The Adventure of the Bruce-Partington Plans"

Whether we term it "New Age thought," or apply such varying labels as "occult," "miraculous," "magical," "unexplained," or some other term, that imprecise category of alleged phenomena commonly designated *supernatural* has fired the popular imagination since earliest times. A sorcerer's communication with spirits of the dead (a power attributed to the biblical "Witch of Endor" for example), or the reputed occult powers of certain objects (the "ancient Mayan" crystal skull, for instance), or a "miraculous" apparition or image (such as that of the Virgin of Guadalupe)—these are termed *supernatural* because they supposedly defy explanation by the known laws of nature. (The term *paranormal* is often used, but in a broader sense so as to include not only the vaguely defined "supernatural" but also such reported anomalies as Bigfoot and extraterrestrials which are as yet unproved but theoretically quite *natural* entities.)[1]

Certainly there is a "New Age" of belief in the supernatural. According to a 1987 survey by the National Opinion Research Council (NORC), two-thirds (67%) of all American adults believe they have had a psychic experience; almost half (42%) think they have contacted the dead (as opposed to only 27% in a 1973 poll); and nearly a third believe they have experienced clairvoyance (31%) or have had visions (29%).[2]

Perhaps not surprisingly, the article reporting the NORC Survey results was followed by one heralding a Hollywood star as a guru of New Age thought:

> One woman more than anyone else, has had the audacity to break the silence and bring the forbidden subject into the limelight. Actress Shirley MacLaine believes that her pals in the spirit world have selected her to "channel" the word of a new/old enlightenment to a skeptical age.[3]

However, the actress's excessive credulity has invited barbs from disbelievers and made her the laughingstock of Johnny Carson's audiences. While we should be open to "new" ideas, we should not wish to become quite as open as, say, a refuse can. Owen S. Rachleff, in his 1971 *The Occult Conceit,* sounded an alarm that seems even more justified today:

> The current craze for the occult suggests, it seems to me, a clear and present danger. This danger is becoming increasingly evident in the widespread proclivity of many immature persons (young and old alike) to govern their lives by the archaic principles of witchcraft and magic, or to conduct their personal affairs and business on the unfounded bases of astrology, numerology, and the Tarot cards.[4]

Many self-styled "investigators" reveal their own excessive credulity concerning such phenomena. A case in point is the so-called ghost-hunter who frequently arrives at the site of an alleged haunting with a reputed "psychic" in tow—the latter's function theoretically being to sense the presence of disembodied spirits. But the reality of such a postulated ability cannot be accepted uncritically, and one cannot explain the unknown by the unproved.

Conversely, the dangers of being too close-minded are illustrated by the example of Jean Bouillaud, a celebrated physician. In 1878 the members of the French Academy of Sciences had gathered to witness the demonstration, by the physicist Du Moncel, of Thomas Edison's recent invention. As the small, primitive phonograph began to speak—faithfully reproducing the words Du Moncel had spoken just moments before—suddenly the 82-year-old Bouillaud leaped at the physicist, grabbing him by the throat. "You wretch!" he shouted. "How dare you try and deceive us with the ridiculous tricks of a ventriloquist!" Bouillaud "knew" that only people—and not machines—could speak.[5]

Some skeptical investigators refer to themselves as "debunkers," which is unfortunate. Although thorough investigation may often result in the debunking of fanciful claims, to call oneself a debunker implies bias, suggesting—rightly or wrongly—that the results are known prior to investigation and will always be negative. This not only lessens the investigator's credibility, but can lead to a habit of mind that too readily accepts a dubious fact simply because it supports a negative position.

Between the two extremes functions the true investigator. To him, or her, mysterious phenomena are not to be uncritically heralded as proof of transcendent realms; neither are they annoyances to be dismissed or debunked at all costs. Instead, to the investigator, mysteries are meant to be *solved.*

A skeptical approach helps guard against the bias of either of the extremes, and objectivity is the hallmark of scholarly and scientific inquiry. One maxim of the investigative approach is that proof should be commensurate with the claim being made: therefore it is held that "extraordinary claims require extraordinary proof." And it should be remembered that the burden of proof (as in a court of law) is on the asserter of fact, on the advocate of the idea in question.

In the case of competing hypotheses, appeals are frequently made to the principle of "Occam's Razor" (after William of Ockham, the fourteenth-century philosopher), which affirms that the simplest explanation that can account for the data—that is, the hypothesis that relies on the fewest assumptions—is most likely to be correct, and is therefore to be preferred.[6]

Predictably, given our backgrounds in research, John Fischer and I have attempted to adhere to just such principles in the investigations comprising this casebook.

John is a forensic analyst in the crime laboratory of the Orange County Sheriff's Office, Orlando, Florida. An experienced crime-scene investigator, he is also president of a corporation specializing in forensic research, especially in the field of laser technology. His specific areas of expertise—including microchemical analyses (for example, those involving blood substances) and instrumental analyses (such as the use of infrared and other spectral analyses)—have proved invaluable in many of our investigations, as has his general scientific approach.

As for me, I have been both a stage magician and a private investigator with an internationally known detective agency, and today I often do investigative writing. ("Artist," "teacher," and "researcher" are among the other labels my frequently changing identity may assume.) For several years I have been a consultant to the Committee for the Scientific Investigation of Claims of the Paranormal (a group formed by such scientists as Carl Sagan and Isaac Asimov).

Since 1978 John and I have shared our complementary skills as a team. (In a fit of good-natured mischief, magician/investigator James Randi once dubbed us Nickell and Dime.) Although we have assisted police departments as well as individuals in matters ranging from death investigations to problems of identity to questions of forged documents, much of our time has been spent on cases involving allegedly supernatural phenomena. Selected examples—including some I investigated alone as well as those on which we collaborated—are treated in the chapters that follow. All began with intriguing questions.

If, for example, there is no preternatural dimension, then what is the source of ghostly footfalls on the stairs of a historic house, especially when they are accompanied by other eerie occurrences and attested to by multiple witnesses?

Or if we do not postulate "spontaneous human combustion"—a phenomenon excluded by known scientific knowledge—how do we account for persons bursting into flame without apparent cause, then being reduced to little more than ashes and bits of bone, while their surroundings remain relatively unscathed?

Without evoking the supernatural, how are we to explain the mysterious disappearance of young Oliver Larch, who went out in the night to fetch water, then vanished suddenly, his tracks in the snow ending abruptly midway to the well?

Although the answers to such questions may disappoint those with preconceived notions of ghosts and magic, others will find that the solutions are often as unique and interesting as the perplexing cases that yielded them. To believer and skeptic alike we say: Join with us in an open-minded approach to the mysteries, accompany us along the trail of evidence, and share in the satisfaction as we begin to unlock the "secrets of the supernatural." Or as Sherlock Holmes would say, "Come, Watson, come! The game is afoot."[7]

Select Bibliography

Edwards, Frank. *Strangest of All*. New York: Signet, 1962. A typical compendium of tales, including that of the disappearance of "Oliver Larch," which supposedly defy scientific explanation but which often fall apart under scrutiny.

Frazier, Kendrick, ed. *Science Confronts the Paranormal*. Buffalo: Prometheus Books, 1986. A collection of skeptical essays and investigative articles by serious researchers, taken from the *Skeptical Inquirer* (the journal of the Committee for the Scientific Investigation of Claims of the Paranormal), and standing in marked contrast to the Edwards approach.

2. HAUNTED STAIRS
The Ghost at Mackenzie House

But are we to give serious attention to such things? This agency stands flat-footed upon the ground, and there it must remain. The world is big enough for us. No ghosts need apply.
—SHERLOCK HOLMES
"The Adventure of the Sussex Vampire"

A century after his death, the ghost of Toronto's rebel-statesman, William Lyon MacKenzie, was not merely going "bump in the night" but, according to several accounts, was also treading noisily upon the stairs of his historic home, plunking the keys of the parlor piano, and even managing to operate his antique printing press—although it was locked and rusting in the cellar![1]

Mackenzie seems a fitting candidate for ghosthood—particularly ghosthood of the restless type—given his turbulent past. Born in 1795 in Scotland, Mackenzie later emigrated to Canada and became a shopkeeper in Toronto (then the town of York). He published the *Colonial Advocate,* a newspaper which served as a vehicle for his attacks against the governing clique. These articles made him a popular hero on the political front, and he was soon elected (1828), then five times re-elected, to the Legislative Assembly of Upper Canada. In 1834 he became Toronto's first civic mayor.

In 1837 Mackenzie led a group of some eight hundred Toronto insurrectionists with the intention of setting up a provisional government. Failing this, he fled to the United States, nearly provoking a war between the two countries before finally being imprisoned (until 1840) for violating American neutrality laws. He eventually succeeded in drawing Britain's attention to colonial abuses, and served again in parliament from 1851 to 1858. He died in 1861 in the now-historic—and supposedly haunted—house on Bond Street (see Figures 1 and 2).

The story of the spooky shenanigans became known in 1960 when Mr. and Mrs. Alex Dobban—who had been caretakers at Mackenzie House for just over a month—told their story to the *Toronto Telegram* and attested to certain ghostly events in sworn statements.

Subsequently, an army pensioner and his wife, Mr. and Mrs. Charles Edmunds, came forward with tales of additional happenings. They had been caretakers of Mackenzie House from August 1956 until April 1960. As Mrs. Edmunds told the *Telegram,* she often saw a woman, or sometimes a small man in a frock coat, standing in her room. For example:

> One night I woke up at midnight to see a lady standing over my bed. She wasn't at the side, but at the head of the bed, leaning over me. There is no room for anyone to stand where she was. The bed is pushed against the wall. She was hanging down like a shadow but I could see her clearly. Something seemed to touch me on the shoulder to wake me up. She had long hair hanging down in front of her shoulders. . . . She had a long narrow face. Then she was gone.[2]

As ghostly occurrences go, however, Mrs. Edmunds's visions are of a type that is all too common. Indeed, they match a phenomenon psychologists term hypnopompic hallucinations. Often described as "waking dreams," such visions are frequently of the ghost-at-the-bedside variety.[3] In fact, Mrs. Edmunds's husband had told her she was dreaming.[4] Yet, in a later statement, he said:

> Another night my wife woke up and woke me. She was upset. She said the lady had hit her. There were three red welts on the left side of her face. They were like finger marks. The next day her eye was bloodshot. Then it turned black and blue. Something had hit her.

Figure 1. Historic home of Canadian rebel-statesman William Lyon Mackenzie (1795-1861), whose ghost reportedly treaded upon the stairs, played the parlor piano, and produced other eerie phenomena.

Figure 2. Sketch made by the author on an early visit to Mackenzie House.

And then, as if anticipating the skeptic, Charles Edmunds insisted: "It wasn't me. I don't think she could have done it herself."[5] Yet who is to say that one of them—tossing fitfully in sleep—did not in fact accidentally strike a swiping blow to Mrs. Edmunds's face?

Subsequent events developed into a full-blown case of what psychologists term "contagion"[6]—a sort of bandwagon effect, which can best be illustrated with the following (non-haunting) example. On December 10, 1978, a small panda escaped from its shelter in the Blijdorp Zoo in Rotterdam, Holland. No sooner did a newspaper report the loss than phone calls began to come in. There were repeated sightings from across the Netherlands, their number underscored by the fact that the panda had actually traveled just 500 meters to a railroad track where it had been killed, presumably by a passing train.[7] As to the panda sightings, probably some persons had seen other animals which they mistook for the missing creature. Others may have perceived a movement out of the corner of the eye and have honestly thought they "saw" what they expected to see. Still other calls may have been pranks or hoaxes.

In the case of Mackenzie House, the Edmunds's visiting grandchildren, ages three and four, were soon claiming they had seen a ghost. After the caretakers moved out, Toronto newspapers hyped the story. *Telegram* reporter Andy MacFarlane and photographer Joe Black gained permission to spend a night in the house, but they were skeptics and experienced nothing.

Nevertheless Archdeacon John Frank of the Holy Trinity Church performed the rites of exorcism in the house, concluding: ". . . Look Down, O Lord, from thy heavenly throne, illuminate the darkness of this night with Thy celestial brightness, and from the sons of light banish the deeds of darkness: through Jesus Christ our Lord. Amen."[8]

In January of the following year, *Fate* magazine carried the story of the alleged haunting. And in 1962, renovations on the house brought reports from workmen who claimed that a sawhorse and dropsheets had been unaccountably moved in the night, although a later break-in and theft seemed less mysterious. Another incident suggested that the workmen, who were obviously caught up in the brouhaha, were playing pranks on each other. One of the men encountered a hangman's noose that had been placed over the stairway.[9]

In 1968 Susy Smith—who would later write of the ghost story at chapter length in her *Ghosts Around the House* (1970)—visited the site.

That was on November 1—or, as she observes, "All Hallows," adding that she had spent Halloween with "a cult of hippie witches." Indeed, she had brought with her to Mackenzie House two "warlocks" known as Raji and J.C. Ms. Smith did admit that the pair "were usually high" on marijuana or hashish, which may explain how they were able to perceive ghosts even when there were none. For example, in descending Mackenzie House's steep staircase, Ms. Smith admitted that she "tripped and nearly fell on my face," but Raji claimed a "demon" had given her a push, while J.C. maintained that "an unseen ghost" was the culprit.[10]

In another instance, Ms. Smith states that "whatever it was . . . knocked my camera off a table . . . and dented it badly. I presumed I had just laid the camera carelessly so that it became overbalanced; but Raji said it was pushed by a demon. J.C. insisted it was an unseen ghost."

Nevertheless, she managed to obtain a spooky picture. The published photo shows Raji with his fingers extended over the keyboard of the antique piano. As Susy Smith herself describes it, it ". . . reveals a mysterious kind of mist between his hands and the keys. If this was caused by double exposure, why is not the rest of the picture in duplicate?"

The answer, of course, is that double exposure was not involved; neither, probably, was camera damage. The answer is so simple and obvious that one would have thought a supposed investigator like Susy Smith could have discovered it. The "mist" is merely the result of glare— or "flashback," as it is sometimes called. The white pages of music resting on the piano simply bounced back her flash, thus washing out a portion of the picture. (As further substantiation, even the dark—albeit polished— wood of the piano shines around the music sheets. And in conjunction, of course, extreme shadows are also present in the print.) I showed the published photograph to a professional photographer, and he concurred with my explanation of the "mist."[11] Susy Smith, however, says nothing about seeking an expert opinion.

Despite an early debunking by the *Star,* the circus atmosphere at Mackenzie House prevailed off and on for some eight years.

In a 1960 editorial, the newspaper attributed the initial reports of ghostly goings-on to the imagination of a publicist for the nonprofit Mackenzie Homestead Foundation. Alex Dobban had said of the ghostly occurrences, according to the newspaper, that there was "nothing to it." He also maintained that his reasons for moving out of the house had

had nothing to do with spooks.[12]

Nevertheless, both the Dobbans and the Edmundses had reported some distinctive phenomena which were also experienced by others. From an investigative standpoint such occurrences are the most interesting because they could indicate some reality beyond dreams, imagination, or hype.

Both Mr. Edmunds and his wife, for example, claimed to hear footsteps on the stairs. As Mr. Edmunds stated, "They were thumping footsteps like someone with heavy boots. This happened frequently when there was no one in the house but us, when we were sitting together upstairs." They also reported peculiar rumbling noises. Their son Robert (who, together with his wife and two small children, lived at the house for a period) described the sound as a rumbling and clanking. He likened it to that made by old printing presses that he had seen in movies. "Not like modern presses," he insisted. Although the younger Edmunds couple heard the "press" but a single time, they maintained that they heard the piano play on some three or four occasions.

During their nerve-wracking tenancy at Mackenzie House, the elder Mrs. Edmunds reportedly lost 40 pounds, and eventually she and her husband moved out. In moved Mr. and Mrs. Dobban, but after scarcely a month they, too, gave up the ghost. As Mrs. Dobban stated in her affidavit:

> We hadn't been here long when I heard footsteps going up the stairs. I called to my husband, but he wasn't there. There was no one else in the house—but I definitely heard feet on the stairs.

She added:

> One night I woke up. There was a rumbling noise in the basement. At first I took it to be the oil burner; but my husband checked and the furnace wasn't on. As it turned out, the noise I heard was the press. It's locked, but I heard it running, not only that night but one or two other nights as well.

She went on to say that another time, when she and her husband had been in bed, she had heard the antique piano playing in the parlor downstairs—not a *tune,* but random plunkings as if a child were playfully hitting on the keys. Robert Edmunds had also heard the weird performance: "I cannot remember what the music was like," he said, "but it was the piano downstairs playing."[13]

Such phenomena invited investigation, and I accepted the challenge during 1972-73 while living in Toronto and working as a professional stage magician. I had been writing a skeptical column on mysterious phenomena—"poltergeists," a spurious "mummy" of a "devil baby," and the like, some of which I had personally begun to investigate—for a magicians' magazine. (At the time I was also studying criminalistics and investigative methods, and would subsequently become a licensed investigator for an international detective agency.)

Before paying a first visit to the house, I searched out published material on the case—old newspaper clippings, books, and magazine articles. In the course of my research I became aware of a surprising lack of concern with the building's environs, all the more so since I had learned that next door to the 82 Bond Street address was Macmillan and Company, the book publishing firm. Could late-night press operations there, I wondered, account for the unexplained rumbling sounds?

The answer, in fact, was no. As my friend, Toronto writer Doug Fetherling, assured me (Macmillan having been his publisher), the building was a combination of offices and warehouse; the printing took place elsewhere. I decided the time had come to see the Mackenzie Homestead firsthand.

Like other visitors, I was greeted by a hostess in period costume who guided me through the narrow dwelling. In the parlor she pointed out an oil portrait of William Lyon Mackenzie, the old family album, and of course the little antique piano. The cellar no longer held the printing press, which had been restored and now reposed, along with Mackenzie's old desk and red leather chair, in a wing added at the rear of the house.

I learned from my guide that caretakers no longer lived there, but that, even so, current policy forbade anyone to spend the night there. I questioned her about her own experiences. She had seen no ghost but in fact *had* heard the mysterious footfalls on the staircase. However, she had managed, on one occasion, to reach the stairs while the phenomenon was still in progress and had learned the source: The sounds were coming from the adjacent Macmillan building.[14] Mackenzie House is separated from Macmillan by only the narrowest walkway. Directly opposite the Mackenzie staircase is a parallel one of Macmillan's. Indeed the latter is made of iron, which amplifies the sound of footsteps—most noticeably those made by the night crew, while caretakers were lying quietly abed thinking of ghosts. According to the hostess, the sense that the footsteps were coming from somewhere within the house was a most convincing illusion.

On a later occasion I visited Macmillan's. In speaking with a receptionist and an editor, I learned that the only printing equipment on the premises was a large mimeograph machine which, although located in a room adjacent to Mackenzie Homestead, was never used at night.

Despite such negative responses, I wanted to talk to the Macmillan building's superintendent. I wondered what he thought of the strange goings-on next door, whether he knew of the part played by the iron staircase in the affair, and whether he had heard the rumbling noises or had any explanation for them.

Luckily, his tenure extended back to the earlier disturbances. As Macmillan personnel introduced him to me, he asked (rather mischievously, I thought) whether I believed in ghosts. I told him I was skeptical, that I believed that most reported ghostly occurrences had rather simple explanations, and that these should be eliminated before we invoked the supernatural. He nodded, but—his eyes twinkling—he stated that he knew one of the Mackenzie House ghosts "personally." If I would return after work in the early evening and ring the bell a specified number of times, he would, he promised, reveal all to my satisfaction. It was an offer I could not refuse.

Shortly before the appointed time, I stood outside Mackenzie House, listening intently. Almost at once I began to hear a faint, distant rumbling—not thunder, but a metallic, machine-like sound not unlike an antique printing press. The sound grew: it was the Dundas Street trolley. I doubted this was actually the source of the reported rumblings, but it did inspire some further thought. Since there was a subway station not far away, I wondered whether the sounds of the underground train might be conducted along sewers or pipes to the celler of Mackenzie House. With that thought in mind, I kept my appointment with the enigmatic custodian.

After greeting me at the door, he led the way into the basement warehouse. Saying somewhat cryptically that he wished to try something, he left me standing at a spot near the Mackenzie cellar while he scurried away. Soon there emerged from the shadows strange noises—eerie whines and clunks and clanks and rumbles. Before long, the "super" was back, wanting to know if I had heard anything mysterious. He explained that he had simply turned on the boiler and—as I had begun to guess— the sounds were caused by the network of expanding pipes.[15]

For his next demonstration, he brought out a large, flat-bedded cart equipped with heavy iron wheels. Loading it with metal garbage cans, as was typically done by the late-night clean-up crew, he pushed it across the warehouse's rough concrete floor. It rumbled and clattered noisily. As the superintendent explained, due to the proximity of the two buildings and their steel underpinnings, the sounds would be telegraphed next door. From the upstairs rooms of the caretakers, *presto:* an antique printing press, surely operated by old Mackenzie himself!

My guide now led me up the offending iron staircase, and explained its proximity to the Mackenzie one, basically corroborating what the hostess there had observed. His was independent confirmation, since I had avoided telling him anything she had said.

I asked about the piano. I had begun to wonder to myself whether the eerie sounds of the expanding or contracting pipes might have seemed—to a suggestible person—like someone plunking, childlike, at the old keyboard. However, I was told that to account for the sounds of the piano we would have to continue on up to the roof.

As it turned out, his family's apartment jutted above the flat expanse of the rest of the Macmillan building. He explained how his son's piano music wafted across the flat roof, struck the taller brick house, and was consequently amplified by a sort of echo-chamber effect caused by the space between the two buildings. Privately, the custodian had determined that such sounds actually seemed louder inside the house due to the effect of the amplification.

My tour ended with the super casually noting a noisy ventilator fan as he led me to his family's quarters. Over a cup of his wife's coffee I heard another little tale concerning the "ghost" of Mackenzie House. One night the custodian was drawn to the rear of the historic dwelling by voices of what turned out to be a group of college kids. Using a listening device which they had placed against the rear wall, they were certain, they told him, that they were hearing spooky manifestations. He donned the earphones, listened briefly, then laughed. "Boys, I hate to tell you, but your 'ghost' is the automatic flush on the men's urinal next door!"[16]

I was left with only one further question for my host. Why, with all the publicity over the alleged haunting, had he not come forward with his own knowledge of the sources of the phenomena? He replied simply that no one—neither self-styled "ghost hunter" nor reporter nor even curiosity seeker—had ever bothered to inquire next door. He had decided, apparently bemusedly, to wait until someone did. It had taken a dozen years.

Select Bibliography

Hervey, Sheila. *Some Canadian Ghosts,* 106–114. Richmond Hill, Ontario: Simon & Schuster of Canada, 1973. A popular account of the Mackenzie House ghost in a compendium of other alleged Canadian hauntings.

Smith, Susy. "Turbulence in Toronto." Chap. 2 in *Ghosts Around the House,* 38-50. New York: The World Publishing Co., 1970. A description of Smith's visit to Mackenzie House in the company of two "warlocks."

Toronto Daily Star. Editorial, 28 June 1960. An early characterization of the supposed haunting of Mackenzie House as a publicity stunt.

Acknowledgments

Material in this chapter appeared in an earlier form as the author's article, "The Ghost at Mackenzie House," *Canada West* (Fall 1979). Special thanks are due the Toronto Historical Board for supplying the photograph of Mackenzie House and giving permission to publish it, and to Linda Quick for seeing that it arrived expeditiously. Additional thanks are extended to Prof. Robert A. Baker, Department of Psychology, University of Kentucky, for reading the chapter in manuscript.

3. GEM OF DEATH
Riddle of the Crystal Skull

I fear, that if the matter is beyond humanity it is certainly beyond me. Yet we must exhaust all natural explanations before we fall back upon such a theory.

—SHERLOCK HOLMES
"The Adventure of the Devil's Foot"

It has been called "the weirdest gem in the world,"[1] and some attribute it to a lost civilization. To those who would see the past and future in its eyes, it is "the granddaddy of all crystal balls."[2] And it is referred to as "the Skull of Doom"[3] by those who believe it holds the power of death over anyone who would mock it.

More commonly known as the Mitchell-Hedges crystal skull, it is a life-sized death's head, fashioned from a single block of natural rock crystal (massive clear quartz) weighing 11 pounds, 7 ounces. Most recent sources—such as Richard M. Garvin's *The Crystal Skull*[4] and Simon Welfare and John Fairley's *Arthur C. Clarke's Mysterious World*[5]— suggest that the sparkling curio first came to light in 1927 during the excavation of a lost Mayan citadel in British Honduras. The adventurer F. A. Mitchell-Hedges participated in the work, and it was supposedly his young adopted daughter, Anna, who found it under an altar of the

---

Investigated with John F. Fischer

ruined city of Lubaantun (from the Mayan word for "place of fallen stones")[6] (see Figure 3).

Mitchell-Hedges mentioned the skull in the first edition of his autobiography, *Danger My Ally* (1954), yet did not specify where or by whom it had been found. He merely published a photograph of what he called "the sinister Skull of Doom," stating in his customarily glib fashion: "It is at least 3,600 years old and according to legend was used by the High Priest of the Maya when performing esoteric rites. It is said that when he willed death with the help of the skull, death invariably followed." Of the skull's provenance, Mitchell-Hedges said only that "How it came into my possession I have reason for not revealing."[7] As if that were not mysterious enough, later editions of *Danger My Ally* omitted all references to the skull, an action which the publishers disclaimed all knowledge of.[8]

To answer the many questions posed by the crystal skull—specifically, Did Anna Mitchell-Hedges indeed find it at Lubaantun or, if not, where did it come from? and, Does the skull actually have the mystical powers ascribed to it?—we began an investigation that was to range over two years. We obtained as much data on the skull as possible: we combed through old newspaper records; corresponded with major museums and laboratories; consulted distinguished experts; amassed information on the Maya, on rock crystal, on the skull motif in art; and sought out those who had examined the skull, as well as Anna Mitchell-Hedges herself.

A starting point was an article by G. M. Morant, "A Morphological Comparison of Two Crystal Skulls," which appeared in a 1936 issue of *Man* (published under the direction of the Royal Anthropological Institute of Great Britain and Ireland). It is the earliest published reference to the Mitchell-Hedges skull, although—intriguingly—it makes no reference to the adventurer; rather, Morant states: "It appears that there are only two life-size representations of the human skull in rock-crystal known to be in existence. One of these is preserved in the Department of Ethnography of the British Museum [where it remains today] and the other is in the possession of Mr. Sydney Burney."[9]

As Morant's comparison of the crystal skulls showed, there are a number of marked differences between the two. The British Museum skull is in a single piece, while the Mitchell-Hedges (or Burney) skull has the lower jaw detached. And in the former, the eye sockets are

Figure 3. The "Skull of Doom," allegedly carved from a block of rock crystal by the ancient Mayans, who supposedly incorporated it into certain of their "esoteric rites." (Photo reproduced from the July 1936 *Man*, at which time the skull was owned by Sidney Burney)

unnaturally circular and the teeth merely indicated, whereas in the latter the eye orbits, teeth, and other details are more anatomically correct.

Still, there are striking similarities, including near-perfect bilateral symmetry and the absence of suture marks, together with certain other features suggesting femaleness in both skulls. By superimposing tracings of the profiles made from photographs, Morant found the correspondence of the two outlines "remarkable." He concluded that it was "impossible to avoid the conclusion that the crystal skulls are not of independent origin. It is almost inconceivable that two artificers, having no connection with one another, and using different human skulls as models, should have produced specimens so closely similar in form as these two are." Morant felt that the two skulls were "representation of the same human skull, though one may have been copied from the other."[10]

A British Museum expert, Adrian Digby, writing in the same issue of *Man,* was not entirely convinced. He did observe that the British Museum specimen was more similar to other crystal skulls, "and therefore more likely to date from Mexican times than Mr. Burney's." He added:

> . . . It is extraordinary that anybody wishing to carve a skull out of rock crystal, and taking a real skull as his model should modify its dimensions to fit those of another crystal skull which he would see was but a poor copy of nature. It shows a perverted ingenuity such as one would expect to find in a forger, but Mr. Burney's skull bears no traces of recent (metal age) workmanship; so this suggestion may almost certainly be dismissed.[11]

However, Frank Dorland, who had the skull on six-years' loan from Miss Mitchell-Hedges for examination, discovered definite "traces of mechanical grinding on the faces of the teeth in the Mitchell-Hedges skull," which he believed were "undoubtedly the work of a treadmill-apparatus commonly employed in the design and crafting of tiny relieved cameos." (Interestingly enough, it is in this same region of the British Museum skull that a powered cutter seems to have been used.) While Dorland believes the skull was "roughed out" by ancient artisans (the Babylonians or Egyptians, he suggests) "by hammering and pressure flaking and then polished," he told us: "Much later the jawpiece was detached and carved and it is only in this piece that any mechanical type grinding is evident."[12]

But Mayan expert Norman Hammond—who has also examined the skull and appeared on a television program with its owner—states: "Miss Mitchell-Hedges said during our Princeton discussion, on camera, that the peg-holes in the skull and jaw were there when she 'found' it. They are clearly the result of drilling with metal, and intended by some previous (?) owner to support the object stably."[13]

A suggestion of mechanical work on the British Museum skull was made in the earliest-known commentary on that specimen. This was by G. F. Kunz, who stated in his classic work *Gems and Precious Stones* (1890) that "the line separating the upper from the lower row of teeth has evidentally been produced by a wheel made to revolve by a string held in the hand, or possibly by a string stretched across a bow, and is very characteristic of Mexican work."* Kunz added: "Little is known of its history and nothing of its origin. It was brought from Mexico by a Spanish officer sometime before the French occupation of Mexico. . . ." (i.e., before 1862).[14]

Kunz's hints of a Mexican origin recall Digby's comment that the British Museum specimen resembled other—supposedly Mexican—crystal skulls. In addition to some rock crystal beads, crescents, and other articles, Kunz mentioned skulls ranging from as small as an inch in width to a half-life-sized one in the Trocadero Museum (now the Musée de l'Homme) in Paris. These are generally classified as Aztec. French experts attribute their specimen to the fourteenth or fifteenth century, and (according to Welfare and Fairley) "To clinch the argument, the French also say that they have found traces of copper tools like those used by the Aztecs on the skull's surface."[15]

As for the British Museum's rock crystal skull, its label states only that it is "possibly of Aztec origin—the Colonial period at the earliest." D. R. Barrett of the Museum's Ethnography Department told us "an Aztec origin has been suggested on grounds of style, but evidence of the possible use of a jeweller's wheel in its carving, if correct, would mean that at least some of the workmanship is of a later date." The museum also has two tiny skulls classified as "ancient Mexican": the smaller of talc and the larger—about 1¼″ high—of rock crystal. Both are perforated and are thought to have been worn as beads or amulets.[16]

---

*No doubt such work would involve an abrasive (as would the drilling of holes—whether the tools were of metal or other material).

We attempted to track down the other small skulls mentioned by Kunz based on his statement that they were (in 1890) in the Blake and Douglas collections.[17] We did learn that the Smithsonian Institution has a list of objects collected in the 1800s by W. R. Blake which refers to eleven small crystal skulls and one much larger one, suggesting that they once composed a necklace. Unfortunately, the skulls were never actually received by the Museum, so this list was the only record that could be found.[18] Nothing further of the skulls' provenance was known, but they bring to mind the "ancient Mexican" skull beads at the British Museum.

Gordon F. Ekholm, Department of Anthropology, American Museum of Natural History, informed us that their collection did have one of the tiny skulls (about 1⅛″ high). Ekholm stated, "It was in the Douglas collection and acquired in 1886, the only data about it being that it comes from the Valley of Mexico—not very helpful." He went on to say,

> I know of various extant skulls of this kind—notably those in the British Museum and in the Musée de l'Homme in Paris. . . . I personally am inclined to doubt that any of them are of Pre-Columbian date—suspecting that they were possibly made during the Colonial period and used as altar pieces. There are other examples that are undoubtedly modern fakes.

He explained that he did not necessarily include the Mitchell-Hedges skull among the fakes, adding, "I suspect that it was probably of an origin similar to that of the British Museum—or that they were probably made sometime during the Colonial period."[19]

The inference in all of this—although largely composed of hints and vague, tentative attributions—is that the various rock crystal skulls that came to light before the Mitchell-Hedges one probably originated in Mexico, no earlier than the Colonial period (i.e., 1519-1821). This is at least consistent with the known frequency of skull depictions in Mexican art (many of which seem to represent Mictlantecutl, the Mexican god of death). These include stone effigies, seals carved in wood, and an actual skull encrusted with a turquoise-and-obsidian mosaic.[20] In his *The Human Skull: A Cultural History* (1966), Folke Henschen observes that skull depictions exist in "lavish profusion" in Mexican culture, whereas there is a distinct scarcity of them in the art of South American civilizations (as there is, incidentally, in the art of North American Indians).[21]

Such stylistic considerations raise grave doubts about the Mitchell-Hedges skull coming from Lubaantun. George Kennedy of the Institute of Geophysics and Planetary Science, UCLA, expressed his skepticism in a letter to Dorland. He explained that the skull is reminiscent of numerous late Aztec objects (carved by Mixtec craftsmen employed by the Aztecs) and—if genuinely pre-Columbian—would have to date from sometime between 1350 and 1500. Kennedy finds it difficult to believe that a late Mixtec object could be found at a Maya site such as Lubaantun, given that that site had been abandoned some six centuries *earlier*.[22] As even Garvin concedes, the crystal skull has been supposed Mayan "only because it was found in Mayan territory."[23] (That is, it was allegedly found there.)

Norman Hammond—who has excavated at Lubaantun and written an admirable, comprehensive, and scholarly monograph on the subject[24] (*Lubaantun: A Classic Maya Realm,* 1975)—is another skeptic. We were struck by the fact that nowhere in Hammond's 428-page book was there any reference to the skull; and little more than a disparaging reference was made to "the 'explorer' F. A. Mitchell-Hedges." But as he explained to us:

> My Lubaantun monograph did not mention the Mitchell-Hedges crystal skull because, of course, the object has nothing to do with the site, or with Maya archaeology (or for that matter, as far as we know, with the pre-Columbian Americas at all). Rock crystal is not found naturally in the Maya area, and there are few if any objects of that material known from Maya sites. The nearest places where it has been found used are Oaxaca (e.g., Monte Alban Tomb 7) and the Valley of Mexico (a few very small crystal skulls such as those in Paris, reputedly of Aztec manufacture).

Regarding Miss Mitchell-Hedges's purported finding of the skull, Hammond states that she "was never at Lubaantun so far as all the documentary evidence shows (including Gann, who would have mentioned her)."[25] Certainly Dr. Thomas Gann omitted the alleged find from his 1931 book, *The History of the Maya.* Neither did he mention the skull in print anywhere else, although he was a prominent member of the expedition.

The same is true of others who were on the expedition, including Captain T. A. Joyce of the British Museum. Mitchell-Hedges's traveling companion, Lady Richmond Brown, who frequently photographed Mitchell-Hedges and his finds, seems never to have photographed the stunning crystal skull or to have included Anna in her Lubaantun photographs. Dr. Hammond adds that "Eric Thompson always called the skull stories fraudulent, and he was at Lubaantun in 1927."[26]

The most profound omission, of course, is that of Mitchell-Hedges himself. So far as is known, he made no reference to the skull at the time of his return from Lubaantun or in the years immediately following. In the 1930s he wrote newspaper articles and a book (*Land of Wonder and Fear*, 1931) that discussed Lubaantun at length, but the remarkable "Skull of Doom" was curiously omitted in favor of relatively humble figurines.

We have already mentioned his claim that he had "reason for not revealing" how he obtained the skull. Lubaantun might be inferred from his mention of the Maya, and yet his statement is difficult to reconcile with Anna's purported finding of the object. After all, the legislative council of British Honduras had granted the explorers sole concession of the then-lost city for a period of twenty years. Mitchell-Hedges wrote that at Lubaantun "thousands of specimens of Mayan culture" were unearthed, adding that "eventually we brought back to England and gave freely to museums in Britain and elsewhere the many specimens we had excavated."[27] Why would there be a special problem with the crystal skull—a reason for not revealing where it came from—if it were indeed found by Anna at Lubaantun?

What we are left with, then—in contrast to the silence of those on the Lubaantun expedition—is the statement of Mitchell-Hedges's adopted daughter that she was the skull's discoverer. Garvin exhibits a photograph of what he terms "an affidavit signed by Anna Mitchell-Hedges attesting to the find." Actually, it is not an affidavit at all, since it is not a sworn statement and bears no notary seal. Rather, it is merely in the form of a simplified letter, addressed to Mr. Dorland and dated 17th February, 1968. In it she states: "The Rock Crystal Skull first appeared during our expedition to Lubaantum [sic] in 1926. We went during 1926, and left before the rainy season in 1927." She adds, in part, "I came upon the skull buried beneath the altar, but it was some three months later before the jaw was found which was about 25 feet away."[28]

Although, at first reading, her initial sentence seems to indicate that the skull was found in 1926, a different interpretation is possible: Garvin states that it occurred "early" in 1927 on Anna's 17th birthday.[29] Welfare and Fairley also accept the 1927 date.[30] Unfortunately for this scenario, however, Mitchell-Hedges wrote in *Danger My Ally,* "Late in 1926 I returned to England from my final visit to Lubaantun."[31] Again, in an article by John Sinclair (*Fate,* March 1962), supposedly based on an interview with Miss Mitchell-Hedges, the finder was given as her father and the date as "in the late 1930s."[32] And Sibley S. Morrill, in his *Ambrose Bierce, F. A. Mitchell-Hedges and the Crystal Skull* (1972), refers to conflicting stories about how Mitchell-Hedges found the skull:

Some stories are that he found it in a Mayan temple on an island off the coast of Honduras. Others have it that the temple was on the Honduran mainland or in Mexico or in British Honduras. And there are yet others that sound as if they originated in the mind of Edgar Rice Burroughs and have about as much fact to support them as the story of Tarzan of the Apes.[33]

In anticipation of resolving these hopelessly conflicting versions, we decided to ask Miss Mitchell-Hedges for clarification. Alas, the web simply became more tangled when she wrote, "My father discovered the Skull in 1924 [sic] in Lubaantun (Place of the fallen stones) during our excavation of that part of Belize" (British Honduras).[34] When we pointed out the obvious discrepancies between that statement and statements in Garvin's book, she offered this explanation:

I did see the skull first—or I saw something shining and called my father—it was his expedition, and we all helped to carefully move the stones. I was let pick it up because I had seen it first. The date 1926-27 in Garvin's book is not correct. In 1924 my father gave it to the Mayans, and when the expedition was completed in 1927 and my father turned the concessions over to the British Museum it was given to Father by the Mayans.[35]

But we have already seen that Mitchell-Hedges was not in British Honduras in 1927. And by repudiating the date in Garvin's book— and thereby disavowing her own "affidavit"—Miss Mitchell-Hedges gives the distinct impression that she has not the slightest idea of when, or even where, the skull was actually found. Regarding her father's silence on the skull's history, she told us: "I know what my father wrote in his autobiography, but as my own autobiography had not been published the actual finding was left to me to tell about. That book is now in the process of being written."[36] We look forward to the next version of the story; in the meantime, we turn again to Anna's soldier-of-fortune foster father in hopes of a clue.

Frederick Albert Mitchell-Hedges, son of John Hedges, was born in 1882 and educated at University College School in London. According to his autobiography, at the age of sixteen he served briefly on a geological survey in the far North. In later years, he alleged, he played poker with J. P. Morgan; drifted about the southern U.S.; claimed various world records for landing giant fish; briefly shared his quarters with a derelict named Bronstein who was to become the Russian revolutionary, Leon Trotsky; and—at gunpoint—joined Pancho Villa's band, participating in the "battle of Laredo."[37]

How much of this is true is anybody's guess. Morrill researched the Laredo incident and found that it never happened—not the saving of the four hundred Villistas by Mitchell-Hedges, nor even the battle itself.[38] Our own doubts about the adventurer were aroused by his 1924 book, *Battles with Giant Fish.* We discovered that the "great white shark" shown in one photo, which he claims weighed "over 1,400 pounds," was identical to one of "two shovel-nose sharks" weighing "1,200 and 1,000 lb."[39]

And so, when we find the adventurer in 1928 losing a libel suit against the London *Daily Express*—which had publicly accused Mitchell-Hedges of staging a fake robbery for self-serving publicity—we may better understand the verdict: The defense, bemoaned the plaintiff in his autobiography, "had developed into an attack on the veracity of my expeditions and my discoveries."[40]

Thus, when Mitchell-Hedges avowed he had "reason for not revealing" how he came to possess the skull, we may wonder what he was up to. And when we find documentary evidence that he *bought the skull in 1944 from a London art dealer,* we may suspect that this is the extent of the deepness and darkness of the secret: The truth was not too sinister to be revealed, but entirely too mundane.

The art dealer was, of course, Sydney Burney, the skull's owner named in the July 1936 issue of *Man.* Previous researchers had assembled valuable details regarding Mitchell-Hedges's purchase, while at the same time arriving at an erroneous conclusion.[41]

The facts are these: In late 1943, Sydney Burney put the crystal skull up for auction at Sotheby's in London; however, when it failed to receive his asking price, it was "bought in" by Burney. A notation in the files of the British Museum, penciled by staff-member H. J. Braunholtz, reads, "Bid at Sotheby's sale, lot 54, 15 × 43 up to £340 (Fairfax). Bought in by Burney. Sold subsequently by Mr. Burney to Mr. Mitchell-Hedges for £400." The sale to Mitchell-Hedges occurred, according to Morrill, in 1944.[42]

Now, Anna Mitchell-Hedges told us that:

> The person who had it [Burney] was holding it for my father and had no right to put it in the auction room at all. The man was a great friend of my father (supposedly) and as we travelled so much it had to be left behind. As soon as my father heard it had been put to auction he was so very very angry he rushed to London and had it withdrawn.

In a later letter she added—repeating what she had told others—that the skull "was left with Mr. Burney as security for a loan to finance an expedition."[43]

However, none of this seems to be supported by the evidence. Morrill cites Adrian Digby as having said that Burney had the skull as early as January 1934 (prior to which time Digby knew nothing of the skull's history).[44] From then until Mitchell-Hedges supposedly reclaimed it is a period of some ten years—during which Burney continued in possession of the skull. That it was "Mr. Burney's skull" at this time is attested to by Digby's statement in his 1936 *Man* article, as well as by Morant, who acknowledged Burney "for permission to handle and measure" the object.[45] And the editors of *Man* published photographs of the skull "By permission of W. Sydney Burney"—not F. A. Mitchell-Hedges.[46] It was obviously still Burney's skull when it was put up for auction in 1943, as it clearly was when he sold it to Mitchell-Hedges shortly thereafter.

As for the skull allegedly being left with Burney as collateral, we must realize that Mitchell-Hedges (according to his autobiography) was in England from 1936 until 1947—except for "a few months" spent on a fishing trip early in that period. (Interestingly, on one unspecified day during that time he casually mentions he "attended a sale at Sotheby's.") Besides, even if the skull had indeed been given as security for a loan, it would appear that Mitchell-Hedges was in a position to have reclaimed it much earlier: In 1936 his financially successful father died, leaving his estate to Mitchell-Hedges, who was thus enabled to move "from Cornwall to a property I had bought in Norfolk, taking with us the collection of silver and other *objets d'art* which my father had left."[47] Surely he could have redeemed the skull from Burney with a tiny portion of his inheritance—had the skull indeed been his to reclaim.

Despite this evidence, we queried his daughter to see if she had any record—such as a letter or newspaper clipping—that might help establish her father's ownership of the skull prior to the Sotheby's auction. Miss Mitchell-Hedges replied that she had "no documentary evidence" before that time, "but," she added, "all my father's papers were lost in Hatteras during a cyclone—photographs and all—also a trunk of his belongings was lost in Plymouth."[48]

Subsequently, there surfaced a document (thanks to Dr. Ekholm) that further discredits Anna's claim that she found the skull at Lubaantun. It is a letter dated March 21, 1933, addressed to George Vaillant of the American Museum of Natural History, written by Sydney Burney, and states: "In answer to your letter of the 10th inst. the Rock-crystal Skull was for several years in the possession of the collector from whom I bought it and he in his turn had it from an Englishman in whose collection it had been also for several years, but beyond that I have not been able to go."

Burney added:

I took it to the British Museum and showed it to Mr. Joyce who was good enough to let me have the Museum's Rock-crystal Skull to compare it with. Captain Gruening, the Lapidary, was there and made a very searching examination of it and found that the method of making and surfaces were precisely the same as those of the Museum [skull]. It was also examined from the anthropological point of view and it was found that the formation of the skull was favourable to its American origin. Its measurements are height 5½ inches and length 8½ inches. I cannot think of any other information to give you but if there are any points which you would like me to answer, would you be good enough to let me know and I will do my best in that direction. I might suggest that if you think it desirable, you communicate with Mr. Joyce at the British Museum on the subject. Apart from its archaeological interest the skull is truly a superb work of art. The price is £1000. (One thousand pounds).[49]

The letter makes it clear that Burney had the skull as early as 1933, that it came from an unnamed collector (seemingly not an English one), and that he had indeed "bought it."

In brief, then, the evidence does not support the claim that the Mitchell-Hedges skull came from Lubaantun. This applies both to its alleged discovery at that site and to the possibility (mentioned by Garvin) that Mitchell-Hedges might have planted the skull there for Anna to find. (Recall his failure to mention the skull in his subsequent writings and his daughter's self-contradictory statements.) Rather, there is convincing evidence that Mitchell-Hedges bought the skull from art dealer Sydney Burney following a 1943 Sotheby's auction.

Realizing that he did so might help explain why references to the skull were deleted from later editions of *Danger My Ally*. No doubt in 1954 (some three years after Sydney Burney's death) there were many persons who could recall Burney's prior ownership of the skull and its sale to Mitchell-Hedges. Might not one such person, angered at what he regarded as deception on the part of Mitchell-Hedges, have threatened exposure?

As for the true origin of the crystal skull, at present we have little more than the object itself, the similar rock crystal skulls in various museums (reputedly of Aztec or Mixtec origin), and the implications of Adrian Digby and Sydney Burney that the skull was understood to have come from Mexico. But as Norman Hammond is quick to point out regarding the supposedly Mexican origin of the various skulls, "Firm evidence is scarce." He says of the Mitchell-Hedges skull:

It is a splendid object, of fine workmanship. I have always thought . . . that it is most likely to have been a *memento mori* [an emblematic reminder of death], of 16th-18th century origin. While a Renaissance origin is not improbable, given the sheer size of the rock crystal block involved manufacture in Qing Dynasty China for a European client cannot be ruled out.[50]

Such alternate (non-Mexican) possibilities gain some support from H. J. Braunholtz of the British Museum, who (also writing in the July 1936 *Man*) commented on the added realism of the Burney skull: "Such realism seems beyond the ordinary range of Aztec art, and gives the skull the character almost of an anatomical study in a scientific age." He cautioned, "In any comparison of these two skulls, this difference of spirit seems to me to be a crucial factor, and one which should be given full weight in drawing conclusions."[51]

We had hoped to conduct an examination of the skull in anticipation of learning more, and had contacted various experts about additional analyses that might be performed. We considered the possibility of identifying the original locale of the rock crystal by comparison with known samples, and also of obtaining an indication of the date of manufacture by means of fluorine diffusion into the surface of the crystal. To this end, we requested permission from the skull's owner, Anna Mitchell-Hedges, for some preliminary tests. We emphasized their non-destructive nature in hopes of forestalling any objections she might make to the removal of even minimal samples. We thought if we could secure her permission for these tests, we might later be able to persuade her to allow the further analyses.

Disappointingly, she refused. She called attention to earlier tests (merely the examinations of Mr. Dorland and one test by Hewlett-Packard that showed that both portions of the skull had been cut from a single large crystal), adding: "I am sorry but I could not let it out of my possession again for testing."[52] And there the matter of the skull's origin rests—uncomfortably—except for a potential clue from Frank Dorland.

Dorland told us that the skull's rock crystal "so closely resembles crystal found in massive deposits in Calaveras County, California, that I suspect that is where the original chunk came from. . . ."[53] Dorland's statement recalls one by Kunz: "It is not known whether the rock crystal used by the aborigines was obtained at a Mexican locality, or whether it came from Calaveras County, Cal., where masses of rock crystal are found containing vermicular procholorite inclusions identical with those observed in the large skull" (now in the British Museum).[54] And it may be worth noting that the American Museum of Natural History has, according to Joe Rothstein of the Department of Mineral Sciences, "a huge quartz sphere that has enough clarity to cut a skull and is from either Calaveras or vicinity."[55]

The final part of our investigation concerned the skull's reputed magical powers. An understanding of these must begin with Mitchell-Hedges himself and be viewed in light of his credibility—or lack thereof. For example, there is his claim that he had found "proof"—off the coast of British Honduras—that the mythical Atlantis had actually been "the cradle of the original American races."[56] His writings are filled with such unfounded, fantastic assertions, and he seems to have been pathologically drawn to exaggeration: In his autobiography, he described the "Skull of Doom" as "dating back at least 3600 years, and taking about 150 years to rub down with sand"; the rock crystal, he exaggerated, was "nearly as hard as diamond." He said further of the skull: "It is stated in legend that it was used by a high priest of the Maya to concentrate on and will death. It is said to be the embodiment of all evil; several people who have cynically laughed at it have died, others have been stricken and become seriously ill."[57] Or so "it is said."

The previously mentioned article by John Sinclair tells what happened to a Zulu witchdoctor and "one of the chief's five wives" after the witchdoctor had "spat at the Skull and performed a mockery dance before it." Mitchell-Hedges had just climbed into his car when "out of a cloudless blue sky a cloud rolled up, thunder crashed and one, and only one, flash of lightning ripped down through the chief's huts," killing the pair.[58]

True? Garvin gives the text of a letter to Mitchell-Hedges which mentions that "members of the Zulu Royal House were struck by lightning," but that sentence begins, "You will have read that. . . ."[59] Therefore, the incident described by Sinclair seems little more than an embellished version in which Mitchell-Hedges is transformed from a reader of the story into an active participant. Moreover, Miss Mitchell-Hedges told us she did not recall having been interviewed for the article, as Sinclair had claimed.[60]

Sinclair also tells the fate of a news photographer who—"not long" after the Zulu incident (and presumably also in South Africa)—sneered at Mitchell-Hedges and defied the skull to will his death: "He walked out of the house with his photographs, climbed into his car and drove head-on into a truck. He was killed on the spot."[61]

Factual? The closest analogy we could find was an undated clipping from an unnamed South African paper (quoted in Garvin). It tells how a newspaper cameraman "within a few hours of photographing the skull" attempted to make a photographic print, whereupon "there was a shattering explosion and the already darkened room was plunged into complete darkness." Apparently the enlarger's bulb had merely burst, but the photographer was quoted as saying, "I ran from the room and nothing would take me back. . . ." Rumors of his death, to paraphrase Mark Twain, seem greatly exaggerated. We share the skepticism of Richard Garvin who says of such stories, ". . . the claims that the crystal skull has caused or can cause death should most likely be filed right next to the curses of old King Tut."[62]

Sinclair makes another fantastic assertion about the skull: "After Mitchell-Hedges said that his tests had shown the temperature of the Skull never changes, other authorities also found that whatever temperature the Skull was subjected to, it maintained a steady temperature of about 70° Fahrenheit. When it was placed in a refrigerator at a temperature of 28° below zero it came out showing a reading of 70°."[63] We know of no supporting evidence that Mitchell-Hedges or "other authorities" ever made such a claim. In any event, it is untrue. As Frank Dorland told us:

> Regarding the claims that the skull maintains a steady 70 degree temperature, that may be true if it is kept in a seventy degree temperature room. Crystal does not change rapidly with heat or cold. It reacts very slowly. Its coefficient of expansion is so low that the bureau of standards often uses crystal as the material to fashion measurement cubes to keep in their vaults. While the skull was in my care (for six years of studies) I detected no abnormal physical differences between it and natural clear quartz crystal.[64]

But if the skull is no different in its physical properties from other rock crystal, what about its mystical properties? Here, Dorland is not exactly a skeptic. He describes at length the strange effects he has experienced while in the skull's presence, sounds as from an "*a capella* choir" and, again, as from "high-pitched silver bells, very quiet but very noticeable." Using it as a crystal ball, he has also seen various images: "other skulls, high mountains, fingers and faces." However, an antique rock-crystal ball he borrowed from a museum "reproduced in a lesser degree," Dorland said, "some of the identical phenomena so outstanding in the Mitchell-Hedges skull."[65] Garvin suggests that these may be only "the result of intense concentration and meditation," adding: "The hypnotic effects the skull transmits—particularly when it is illuminated [as by candlelight]—could easily induce trance states to easily susceptible or sensitive persons." Garvin was himself unable to see or experience any of the phenomena, and an "aura" Dorland had once seen surrounding the skull could be represented only in a "simulated photograph."[66] Possibly the phenomena must be believed to be seen.

In any case, perhaps it is enough to point out that similar phenomena can be experienced under similar meditative conditions. (For an interesting discussion of crystal balls and their effects we recommend Kunz's *The Curious Lore of Precious Stones.*[67])

Anna Mitchell-Hedges told us, "The skull has been used for healing a number of times, and I hope one day it will go to an institution where it will be used by mathmaticians [sic], weather people, surgeons, etc., etc."[68] But we suspect that all such notions of the skull's mysterious powers are attributable to the shimmering patterns of light and shadow that play upon its polished contours, made all the more eerie by its grinning visage. Add to this the superb quality of its workmanship and the uncertainties about its exact origin, and we understand why it continues to fascinate. The skull deserves no mockery—unlike many of the claims made about it.

Select Bibliography

Garvin, Richard. *The Crystal Skull.* Garden City, N.Y.: Doubleday, 1973. A popular, book-length treatment of the Mitchell-Hedges crystal skull, not without some skepticism of the more outlandish claims.

Kunz, George Frederick. *Gems and Precious Stones,* 285-286. New York: Scientific Publishing Co., 1890. An early mention of the British Museum crystal skull and other smaller skulls of possibly Mexican origin.

Mitchell-Hedges, F. A. *Danger My Ally,* 243. London: Elek Books, 1954. The first edition of Mitchell-Hedges's autobiography with brief, cryptic statements about the skull and its reputed power to cause death.

Morant, G. M. "A Morphological Comparison of Two Crystal Skulls." *Man* 36 (July 1936): 105-107. A detailed comparison of the Mitchell-Hedges crystal skull with the one in the British Museum.

Morrill, Sibley S. *Ambrose Bierce. F. A. Mitchell-Hedges and the Crystal Skull.* San Francisco: Caledon Press, 1972. Despite some useful information, a far-fetched scenario involving the crystal skull, the disappearance of American writer Ambrose Bierce (who was supposedly a secret agent along with Mitchell-Hedges), and other disparate elements.

Sinclair, John. "Crystal Skull of Doom." *Fate,* March 1962, 64-68. A silly article that touts unfounded claims about the crystal skull's supposed magic powers.

Welfare, Simon, and John Fairley. *Arthur C. Clarke's Mysterious World.* New York: A & W Publishers, 1980. An account mentioning Mitchell-Hedges's purchase of the skull from an art dealer, but without pursuing the full implications of that fact.

Acknowledgments

This chapter first appeared as "Crystal Skull of Death" in *Fate* magazine (July and August issues, 1984), to whose editors we are grateful for permission to reprint it.

We also extend thanks to the individuals and institutions mentioned in the text and references—particularly to Mayan expert Norman Hammond, and to Gordon F. Ekholm of the American Museum of Natural History—for their invaluable assistance.

4. PHANTOM PICTURES
Self-portraits of the Dead

*Chance has put in our way a most singular and whimsical problem,
and its solution is its own reward.*

—SHERLOCK HOLMES
"The Man with the Twisted Lip"

Stories of "mediums" who could communicate with spirits of the dead
are quite ancient—a biblical example being the account of the Witch
of Endor, who had a "familiar spirit" and who, at King Saul's behest,
conjured up the ghost of Samuel (I Samuel 28:7-20).

The practice was given new impetus in 1848 by the activities of
two young girls, daughters of a Methodist farmer named John Fox,
in northern New York state. Using trickery (to which the girls confessed
many years later), Maggie and Katie Fox produced rapping noises that
they attributed to the ghost of a murdered peddler. Assisted by the
promotion skills of their older sister, Mrs. Leah Fish, the girls demonstrated their apparent ability to contact other spirits as well, all of whom
answered questions by means of raps during "séances." After successful
demonstrations in New York City, the girls traveled all over the country
promoting their "Spiritualist" society.[1]

Within six years, spiritualism had attracted such interest that there

---

Investigated with John F. Fischer.

were no fewer than 15,000 signatures on a petition to the U.S. Senate calling for a government investigation.[2] The believers urged this because, they said, the dead were anxious to communicate with the living. Nevertheless, the petition was tabled.

In the meantime, "spirits" began producing a variety of strange phenomena at séances featuring the Davenport Brothers, William Henry and Ira Erastus. While the young brothers were apparently securely tied to chairs, spirits allegedly caused guitars to strum and tambourines to rattle; occasionally, despite the near-darkness of the performance halls, spectators would even glimpse an eerie hand. The brothers traveled throughout the United States by stagecoach and river steamers, and after several years toured Europe, where they had several run-ins with professional magicians and other skeptics. (In an English burlesque of their show, an actor made up as the brothers' lecturer, a Reverend Ferguson, quipped: "Many sensible and intelligent individuals seem to think that the requirement of darkness seems to infer trickery. So it does. But I will strive to convince you that it does not.") Years later, after many more American performances, Ira Davenport explained to magician Harry Houdini how the brothers got in and out of their ropes so they could produce the spirit phenomena.[3]

Despite endorsements by such respected persons as scientist William Crookes (and later by the writer, Sir Arthur Conan Doyle), the growing cult of spiritualism was continually plagued by accusations of fraud. For example, in 1876, after a spiritualist medium had "materialized" the body of her "spirit guide" (an Indian named "Sunflower"), a reporter discovered the medium's accomplice hidden in a recess.[4]

Daniel Dunglas Home (pronounced Hume) is sometimes represented as "the medium who was never exposed," but this is largely attributable to the fact that he avoided performing publicly. Instead, he took advantage of his credulous hosts, who showered him with expensive gifts and allowed him to contrive the conditions in which he worked his apparent wonders. Many—including Robert Browning—did, however, observe what they maintained were deceptive practices on the part of Home, and the fact that many of his feats suspiciously resembled standard magic tricks and side-show stunts adds to the case against him.[5]

Nowhere was trickery more prevalent than in the production of otherworldly photography. As early as 1861, a Boston engraver named William H. Mumler had been producing alleged spirit photos (see Figure 4), but

W. H. MUMLER.

MRS. W. H. MUMLER.—BY MUMLER.

SPIRIT PHOTOGRAPH BY MUMLER.

SPIRIT PHOTOGRAPH BY MUMLER.

Figure 4. Engravings show the "spirit" photographer, Mumler, and some of his bogus productions. (From the May 8, 1869, *Harper's Weekly;* Author's collection.)

he was suspected when some of the "spirits" were recognized as living Bostonians. Similarly, the trickery of a British medium named Hudson was uncovered in the 1870s when photographers discovered that some of the spirits he photographed were actually Hudson himself in disguise, and that many of the pictures were double exposures.[6]

As recently as 1964, fraudulent spirit pictures were being produced at a spiritualist "church" in Connecticut. In the darkened séance room, sitters prayed and concentrated on squares of photographic paper held in their hands. After developing the paper in trays of chemical solutions provided for the purpose, sitters saw faces appear on the squares. Unfortunately, investigation by magician James Randi revealed that these had been faked by using pre-exposed photographic negatives. The sitters— who were expected to "donate" $20 to $30 at each meeting—were merely victims of what Randi termed a "racket."[7]

Somewhat similar fakery involving what is called "spirit precipitations on silk" has taken place at the infamous Camp Chesterfield in Chesterfield, Indiana. Following an initial exposé of that spiritualist camp in 1960— infrared film having revealed that "the ghosts were living people masquerading in luminous clothes"[8]—a further bombshell came in 1976. It was delivered by M. Lamar Keene, a former fraudulent medium at Camp Chesterfield, who exposed the "psychic sideshow" there in his book, *The Psychic Mafia.*[9]

Saying that money was "the name of the game," Keene told how the damning infrared film footage of 1960 (showing "spirits" using a secret door) was explained to the credulous: "It was all 'trick photography,' we told our people, and of course the spirit communicators backed us up in our séances. That was good enough for our followers!"[10]

In a chapter titled "Secrets of the Séance," Keene detailed the tricks used by mediums at Camp Chesterfield, as well as at Camp Silver Belle (in Pennsylvania), and elsewhere. He told how "apports" (said to be gifts from the spirits) were purchased and hidden; how chiffon or gauze became "ectoplasm" (an imagined mediumistic substance); how written questions placed in sealed envelopes were secretly read and then answered; and how trumpets were made to "float" and fake spirits to materialize.[11]

Our own encounter with spirit pictures began in mid-1985 when we were given a swatch of cloth bearing what were purported to be supernaturally produced portraits of "spirit guides." On behalf of the cloth's owner, we were asked to investigate the possibility that the spirit pictures were fraudulent, and later the owner made a sworn affidavit containing particulars of the séance at which the pictures had supposedly materialized. We also obtained a statement from other informants who were disgruntled at what they regarded as a con game.[12]

These informants had been members of a "higher consciousness" group that dabbled in mystical phenomena, and a medium from a spiritualist camp had conducted several séances for them at the private home of the group's leaders, a young couple.

One séance involved the production of "apports"; another featured supposed "materializations" of spirits. To insure darkness, the windows and doors had been covered with aluminum foil and black plastic garbage bags (apparently with no symbolism intended).

The séance involving the spirit pictures took place on an April evening, and was attended by about forty persons. Apparently, this was greater than the number expected, and one person was reportedly turned away "because there were no more silks" (actually pieces of synthetic fabric). This is interesting in light of the fact that the hostess had some white cloth that she had volunteered for the occasion.

As people arrived, they were assigned a seat and given a sheet of construction paper; these were to place the "silks" on later, supposedly to keep the ink that would be used from staining the participants' clothes. The medium emphasized keeping the swatch of cloth on top of the paper, face down. At this point, the hostess collected $20 in cash from each person (the total would have been about $800).

The medium now made his entrance and held a "spirit trumpet" under a lamp so that a phosphorescent band on it would become luminous in the dark; this allowed the participants to see it apparently float about the darkened room while spirits allegedly spoke through it. Also incorporated into the activities that followed were an open bottle of black ink which the spirits would theoretically use to make the pictures; a stack of seemingly blank cloth squares; and a low-wattage, red-light lamp such as photographers use.

The red light was switched on after the other lights were turned off. The result was that the medium—who now passed out the cloth squares—could not be seen, even from a few feet away. "The dimness of the red light," states one informant, "caused a cloudy, relaxed effect on the eye, making it hard to distinguish detail." He adds, "This, of course, gives way to creative visualizations, such as seeing ectoplasm."

To ensure that darkness would be maintained, the medium warned the participants that he would die instantly if anyone so much as flicked on a cigarette lighter.

As we were told: "The remainder of the séance, [the medium] went into [a] trance and the trumpets gave messages and danced, while the group held their silks by the edges on a piece of construction paper in our laps. This is a group participation thing, as we were told to sing and to concentrate and use our energies." Participants were also told they might actually feel spirits tugging at the cloths.

Some of the attendees became suspicious of the alleged "spirit" voices, however, when they noted that the "voices" were always male and sounded just like the medium's own—complete with grammatical errors characteristic of his speech. Also, the messages were "quite often the same, sometimes meaningless messages as of previous séances," we were informed.

Later—after the medium had taken the red light from person to person, and had had each turn over his or her cloth in order to reveal the spirit pictures—our informants also became suspicious of the images. Although participants had been instructed to roll up the cloths in the construction paper in order to keep them from being handled or exposed to the light for twelve hours and to prevent smearing or fading of the images, two of our informants opened theirs when they got home. Not only did handling and exposure to the light have no adverse effect on the images, but these looked suspiciously like photographs from newspapers. Moreover, no additional faces had appeared on the cloths—as had been said might occur—although it was rumored that one person at the séance had become convinced that that had happened with his cloth. However, since the images were viewed in the near-dark (in which a relatively light image might not be seen), and since the 12-hour interval might cause one to forget just how many images had aotually been on his or her cloth (the number varied on the different cloths), such an occurrence would be difficult, if not impossible, to prove.

We procured one of the cloths taken home from the séance (see Figure 5) and showed it to Robert H. van Outer, a photography expert at the University of Kentucky Photographic Services, who assisted us throughout our investigation. It was his professional opinion that the images were probably transferred onto the cloth from newspaper or magazine pictures.[13]

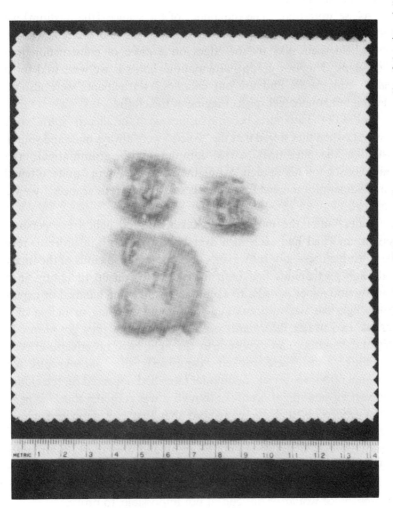

Figure 5. Alleged "spirit precipitations" on cloth, produced at a 1985 séance. Images are supposedly of the sitters' "spirit guides."

A similar view was expressed by a spokesman for a firm that imprints pictures and designs onto textile products. He thought that the images were transfers of some sort made from printed pictures.[14]

Subsequently, we subjected the cloth to a series of essentially nondestructive tests. Preliminary visual examination showed similarities between the three images and ordinary photographic images. The clarity, tonal gradations, and arrangements of highlights and shadows on the cloth are in fact quite common in photos of real, three-dimensional objects exposed to a directional light source. (There is even a partial shadow area behind one figure.)

The softened outer edges of the images do not resemble the vignetting found in some commercial photographic portraiture, but they do exhibit an unevenness and seeming directionality that is distinctive and can result from some transfer processes. Additionally, there were no visible brush-strokes or appreciable concentrations of pigment. Neither were there observable signs of "bleeding" into the threads by liquid ink, dye, or the like. In fact, viewed from the reverse, there was no saturation, and indeed show-through was minimal. The overall effect was of a dry or semi-dry image-forming process. Background (i.e., non-image) areas of the cloth showed no noticeable traces of photo-emulsion or other such foreign substances.

A polarized-light microscopic examination of the cloth and its images revealed that the coloring matter had not been applied in a fluid medium (e.g., india ink, paint); instead its appearance matched that of images transferred from an image-bearing surface such as a newspaper page. (Although no halftone dots were detected, their presence was precluded by the greater coarseness of the cloth, as we learned by experimentation on comparable fabrics). This also meant that if any liquid had been involved in the transfer process, it did not actually dissolve the colorant. Examination of the background areas under the microscope revealed no significant foreign substances, such as photographic emulsion, gels, pastes, or similar material.

The cloth was also examined using an extended infrared video system, and shortwave and longwave ultraviolet light. Various chemical tests were also conducted. Iron-gallotannate, logwood, nigrosine, and aniline ink, as well as ballpoint and many other common kinds of ink, were all eliminated from the list of possibilities by these analyses; however, the coloring matter was indistinguishable from a printers' ink used for comparison in all the tests.

Finally, viewing under argon-ion laser light (see Figure 6) indicated the presence of a randomly dispersed fluorescer. Prominent circular areas (which had been barely visible under longwave UV) were clearly observed to surround each image (see Figure 7). These areas were mostly devoid of the fluorescer, which had been dissolved by a liquid (since evaporated) and carried to the margins of the "stain." This suggests the application of a liquid such as that used in an image-transfer process. (Experimentation showed that alcohol—but not certain other liquids—will produce the identical effect.)[15]

Not only did the analyses point to a transfer process, but so did the reported conditions under which the squares of cloth were passed out and the images revealed, which allowed the cloths to have had images placed on them before the séance.

That the cloths were indeed prepared in advance is also supported by the medium's expressed concern that he might not have enough squares to go around even though there was a quantity of additional white cloth available to him at the time. Prior preparation of the cloths is further suggested by the manner in which the participants were instructed to handle the squares (to keep them face down), and is underscored by the fact that bogus "spirit" pictures—involving just such prior preparation of the cloths with images transferred from printed photos—are known to have been produced at spiritualist camps. In *The Psychic Mafia,* Keene tells how "spirit precipitation" was accomplished:

> The trick here was to prepare the silks in advance. I used to cut pictures out of old magazines or use snapshots of spirits known to the sitters if I had them, soak the picture in ammonia for thirty seconds, place it on bridal silk, put a handkerchief over it, and use a hot iron. The image impregnated the silk.[16]

Sometimes, anticipating skeptics, Keene would have sitters sign their pieces of "silk" (which was often satin), have the silks secretly removed and prepared by confederates in an adjacent room, and then have them returned before the séance ended. Keene continues:

> Once at Camp Chesterfield, while doing precipitations, I got lazy or careless or both and caused a minor crisis. Sick of cutting out and

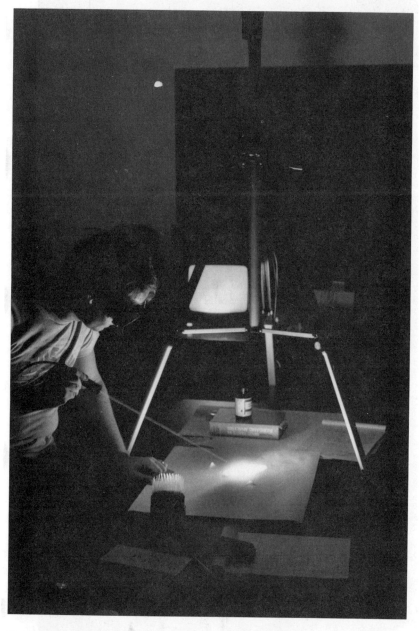

Figure 6. Forensic analyst John F. Fischer examining evidence with the argon laser. This coherent light can reveal traces invisible to the unaided eye.

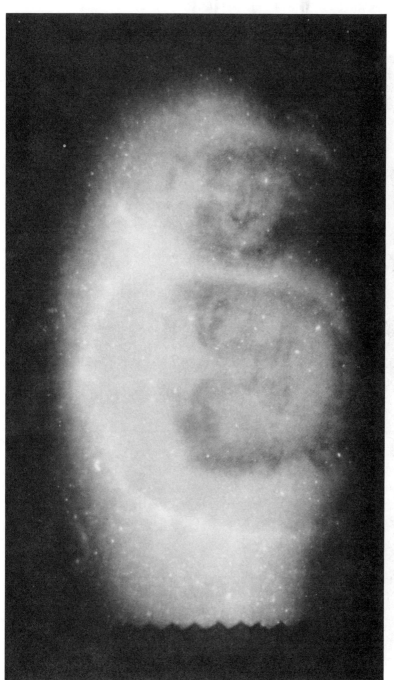

Figure 7. Laser light reveals telltale solvent-produced areas around "spirit images."

ironing the damn things, I used any picture that was handy, one of a little girl on a recent cover of *Life* magazine. The woman who got the silk recognized the picture and went to Mamie Schultz Brown, the president of the camp that year. Mamie was very excitable; she almost fainted when the woman confronted her with the silk and the incriminating picture from *Life*.

"However," Keene added, "we smoothed it over by telling the woman that sometimes the spirits did mischievous things like that just to remind us they were still human and liked a joke."[17]

Because of the possibility of exposure, says Keene, one experienced medium advised against giving out apports or spirit pictures or anything "that could possibly be used in court as tangible evidence against us." But most mediums, he added, felt they were protected by "the wall of fanatical credulity that our followers had built around us."[18]

Using the information gleaned from the various analyses and experiments, we were able to simulate convincingly the image-forming process on similar cloth. (Our technique, a variant of the Keene recipe, involved placing a square of polyester cloth over a newspaper photo, moistening the cloth with alcohol, and rubbing it firmly with a burnishing tool.) We easily made a quantity of such prepared cloths (a few images to a square), one of which is shown in Figure 8.

At this writing, the medium who conducted the séances with the fake spirit pictures and other phenomena—perhaps learning of the subsequent activities of a few disillusioned participants—has failed to return to the city where he initially found such a warm reception. Should he chance that way again, however, police warrants charging him with "theft by deception" are waiting to offer him a different kind of welcome.

Select Bibliography

Christopher, Milbourne. *ESP, Seers and Psychics: What the Occult Really Is.* New York: Crowell, 1970. A thoroughly skeptical look at the "occult" world (with chapters on famous mediums and related phenomena like table tilting, plus a bibliography) by the former head of the Occult Investigating Committee of the Society of American Magicians.

Hunt, Douglas. "Spiritualism." Chap. 1 in *Exploring the Occult,* 16–34. New York: Ballantine, 1964. An overview of spiritualism by a credulous British

Figure 8. Images experimentally produced by author replicate "spirit" pictures.

schoolmaster who is nevertheless aware that much deception occurs.

Keene, M. Lamar (as told to Allen Spraggett). *The Psychic Mafia.* New York: St. Martin, 1976. A devastating exposé of spiritualist frauds by a former practitioner, who reveals many tricks including a method of producing "spirit precipitations on silk."

Mulholland, John. *Beware Familiar Spirits.* 1938. Reprint. New York: Scribner, 1979. A stage magician's debunking of such mediumistic phenomena as apport production, slate writing, and spirit photography.

Randi, James. "A Skotography Scam Exposed." *Skeptical Inquirer* 7, no. 1 (Fall 1982): 59-61. A firsthand report by a noted magician and paranormal investigator on fake spirit pictures produced on squares of photographic paper.

Smith, Susy. *Widespread Psychic Wonders.* New York: Ace Publishing, 1970. An overly credulous look at such "occult" topics as spiritualism, telepathy, ghosts, and possession.

Acknowledgments

We extend our sincere thanks to Robert H. van Outer, University of Kentucky Photographic Services, and to Debbie Fischer, Orlando, Florida, for their generous help with various aspects of this investigation.

5. VANISHED!
Incredible Disappearances

*Among these unfinished tales is that of Mr. James Phillimore, who,
stepping back into his own house to get his umbrella, was never more
seen in this world.*

—DR. WATSON
"The Problem of Thor Bridge"

In his *Strangest of All* Frank Edwards asks: "Is it possible for a human
being to walk off the earth? Science says that it is not, but if that is
correct, then what happened to Oliver Larch?"[1]

According to Edwards, the Larch family farmhouse stood on the
outskirts of South Bend, Indiana. It was Christmas Eve, 1889, and a
snowfall was accumulating. While the Larch family, their minister, and
some friends were in the parlor singing to Mrs. Larch's organ music,
eleven-year-old Oliver was in the kitchen popping popcorn.

Shortly before eleven o'clock Oliver's father asked him to go to
the well for water. But no sooner had the lad slipped on his overshoes
and started on his errand than the adults heard his frantic screams:
"Help! Help!" he cried. "They've got me! Help! Help! Help!"

The adults rushed outside, with Oliver's father carrying a kerosene
lamp. The youth's cries were already beginning to grow fainter, but—
the witnesses would afterward agree—they seemed to come from the

Figure 9. "There were no other marks of any kind in the soft snow. Just Oliver's footprints . . . and the bucket . . . and silence."

blackness overhead! Lamplight revealed that the boy's tracks led about halfway to the well and then ended abruptly! According to Edwards, "There were no other marks of any kind in the soft snow. Just Oliver's footprints . . . and the bucket . . . and silence" (see Figure 9). He adds that subsequent investigation proved the truth of the story. Neither eagles nor even a balloon, he argues, could have made off with the frightened boy. And he concludes, "Because it defied logical explanation, the disappearance of this boy was quietly filed away and forgotten."[2]

Intrigued by the story, I began an investigation of the matter in May of 1979. My approach was two-pronged: I sent off inquiries in hopes of verifying the incident, and in the meantime I formulated a hypothesis. Possibly, I reasoned, Oliver had simply fallen in the well! An experienced accoustics professional verified that sounds coming from a well would indeed be projected upward and under certain conditions could be heard as reported. I speculated that the lad could have exhibited typical eleven-year-old boyish behavior, possibly making his way to the well in some playful manner—say along a clothesline or nearby fence (thereby leaving no footprints)—and had thus arrived at the well in a precarious manner, resulting in his falling in. Naturally, the boy's cries would have become weaker as he grew more and more tired, until he eventually slipped under the surface of the water.

I discussed the case with Tom McDonald, chief investigator for the medical examiner's office in Orlando, Florida. Mr. McDonald pointed out that the well-water could have remained at or below morgue temperature year-round. Therefore *if* we assumed that after the drowned body sank it somehow became trapped at the bottom of the well (or if it was carried away by an underground stream), it was possible—just possible—that the fact would never have become apparent. Of course, while such a scenario would seem capable of accounting for the alleged facts in the case, it was nonetheless purely speculative and McDonald agreed that—until it could be verified—the story should be taken with the proverbial grain of salt.[3]

Mr. Edwards's publishers were unable to provide any source reference for the tale; so, apparently, was his widow, who did not reply to my letter. However, I received an earlier version of the story courtesy of Mary Margaret Fuller, editor of *Fate* magazine (for which Edwards had once been a contributing editor). According to the 1950 article in *Fate* by Joseph Rosenberger, young Oliver *Lerch* also disappeared while on an errand to the family well. His cries seemed to come from overhead and his tracks ended abruptly midway to the well. But there were differences between the Rosenberger and Edwards versions: Oliver Lerch was *twenty* years old and the event took place in *1890;* moreover, the distance to the Lerch well was six times greater than that to the Larch one—an amazing 450 feet.[4]

Which was the real Oliver—Larch or Lerch? Neither, answer Indiana researchers. An exhaustive search of local records was made at my request by Glen L. Terry, Chief of the Services Division, South Bend Police Department, and by Dr. Loyal E. Fields of the Northern Indiana Historical Society. No record of any Larch *or* Lerch disappearance was found in the police files (as the *Fate* article had alleged): neither was such an incident reported in contemporary newspaper accounts: nor, finally, was there any evidence in census records, city and county directories, or other sources[5] of a Larch or Lerch family living in the South Bend area during the 1880s or '90s.

What did turn up were some relatively recent clippings on the purported incident from the local newspaper. These in turn mentioned speculations that the "disappearance" might have resulted from a flying saucer kidnapping, with one reporter claiming that next to Oliver's footprints had been the tracks of "little men." According to the *South Bend Tribune,* "The legend of Lerch was launched in 1949 [or 1946, reads another clipping] by a radio show."[6]

But maybe the lad's name was Oliver *Thomas;* the year, 1909; and the place Rhayader, Wales!—as reported by Brad Steiger in his *Strangers from the Sky* (1966).[7] Again it was Christmas Eve and the Thomas lad had stepped outside. . . .I wrote to the Rhayader mayor, Eddie Collard, and he in turn inquired of the townsfolk and police. As a result, Mayor Collard concluded that the Thomas story was a hoax. Rhayader residents, he said, had only heard the astonishing tale from Mr. Steiger's book.[8]

The "Lerch" version seems to be the earliest one. Eventually I developed a suspect in the hoax, tracked him to his present address, and confronted him with my suspicions. He replied, "OK. There is not a single bit of truth to the 'Oliver Lerch' tale. Every single bit is fiction. I wrote the damn piece way back when during the lean days. . . . It was all fiction for a buck."[9]

The basic story, however, bears obvious similarities to an Ambrose Bierce short story titled "Charles Ashmore's Trail" (in *Can Such Things Be?* originally published in 1893). According to this story, the Christian Ashmore family resided near Quincy, Illinois. On a November evening in 1878, sixteen-year-old Charles "left the family circle about the hearth" and went to a spring for water. When the youth failed to return, his father "lighted a lantern" and, accompanied by his eldest daughter, went in search. But "the trail of the young man had abruptly ended, and all beyond was smooth, unbroken snow."

A few days later, so the story goes, in passing the spot where her son's tracks had ended, Mrs. Ashmore heard her son's voice. Bierce continues:

> . . . For months afterward, at irregular intervals of a few days, the voice was heard by several members of the family, and by others. All declared it unmistakably the voice of Charles Ashmore; all agreed that it seemed to come from a great distance, faintly, yet with entire distinctness of articulation; yet none could determine its direction nor

repeat its words. The intervals of silence grew longer and longer, the voice fainter and farther, and by midsummer it was heard no more.[10]

Because of the obvious similarities between the "Lerch" legend and the "Ashmore" one, I inquired again of the self-confessed "Lerch" hoaxer. He replied, "To the best of my knowledge, I have never read Bierce's *Can Such Things Be?* . . . I do wish I could be of further help to you. It is possible that other writers had similar story lines . . . [and] that I heard/read . . . something similar to the 'Lerch' story and then did one of my own." He concluded, "As far as I recall, the name 'Oliver Lerch' is pure fiction on my part."[11] I reported this qualified confession in the March 1980 issue of *Fate* (withholding the author's name at his request).[12]

Later, however, I learned of a booklet by Harold T. Wilkins, published in 1948,[13] which indicated that the basic tracks-in-the-snow story—with the "Oliver Lerch" name affixed—was current well before 1932. Therefore, the confession of the putative hoaxer meant little, except to indicate that (as he admitted) he had a poor memory. It now seems that he had merely passed along a story which he already knew (or at least suspected) was untrue, making some very minor alterations.

Other versions of the tracks-in-the-snow story are known. A detective story (published in 1928) relates how "James Settle," a coachman, vanished from his New York farm after going to the barn to feed his horses. A more recent spin-off transforms Bierce's "Charles Ashmore" into "Charl*otte* Ash*ton*" and sets the disappearance in London in 1876.[14] These stories are linked by the common motifs: the eerie cries and the abruptly ending tracks.

So much for the tracks-in-the-snow story. But then whatever happened to David Lang? As Robert Schadewald summarized the story, Lang supposedly vanished in broad daylight in full view of witnesses:

On the afternoon of September 23, 1880, a Tennessee farmer named David Lang stepped off the face of the earth. He walked into his pasture to look at his horses and with his wife and children and friend Judge August Peck looking on, he vanished! The stunned onlookers rushed to the spot where he was last seen but could not find a trace of him. There was no hole in the ground, no subterranean cave, nothing to explain his disappearance. He was just gone. It was reported that as

> time passed a circle of stunted yellow grass grew at the spot where David Lang disappeared and sometimes members of the family could hear his voice calling weakly for help from inside the circle.[15]

A number of books and magazines—including the *People's Almanac*—have accepted the story as true.[16]

Nashville librarian Hershel G. Payne investigated the Lang story and reports that, although he checked census and other records, there was "nothing to indicate that David Lang or Judge Peck were ever in this vicinity." Payne adds that other knowledgeable persons, including the Sumner County historian, "also attest to the story's fictitiousness."[17]

But if these findings are correct, and there was no David Lang, how do we explain the existence of his daughter, Sarah Emma Lang? A firstperson account by Miss Lang was published under the byline of Stuart Palmer in the July 1953 issue of *Fate* in an article titled "How Lost Was My Father?" An accompanying affidavit was signed by Miss Lang and witnessed by Palmer. Additionally, it bore the signature of a New York notary.

Sarah Lang deposed that she had been eleven years old when the fantastic incident transpired. She said that her mother had collapsed immediately and that her mother's hair had soon turned white. Sarah further claimed that she and her brother had once heard their father calling for help from within the circle of grass. After failed attempts to contact her father through spiritualist mediums, Sarah eventually took up "automatic writing" and finally received a message from her father. She claimed that the handwriting was indeed his.[18]

But Schadewald became suspicious of the affidavit when he noticed that it did not bear the notary's seal. Consulting a handwriting expert, Ann B. Hooten of Minneapolis, Schadewald provided her with reproductions of the automatic writing and affidavit. Mrs. Hooten's analysis of the handwriting led her to conclude that it had been disguised and that "all the accumulated writings were authored by one individual."[19]

In summary, then, the Lang disappearance was a hoax and the later writings and affidavit were fraudulent. Sarah Lang, therefore, like her supposed father, was fictitious.

Schadewald notes the obvious similarities between the Lang yarn and another of Ambrose Bierce's short stories, "The Difficulty of Crossing a Field." This was one of a trilogy (including "Charles Ashmore's Trail" plus "An Unfinished Race") grouped under the heading "Mysterious Disappearances" in his *Can Such Things Be?*

"The Difficulty of Crossing a Field" tells the incredible story of a "planter named Williamson" who lived in the vicinity of Selma, Alabama. One July morning in 1854, the story goes, Williamson strolled down his walk, and, plucking a flower, crossed the road into his pasture. Then— witnessed by his wife and a passing neighbor, Armour Wren—he vanished. To the question asked by Wren's young son, "What has become of Mr. Williamson?", Bierce says wryly, "It is not the purpose of this narrative to answer that question." He then "quotes" from "Mr. Wren's strange account of the matter, given under oath in the course of legal proceedings relating to the Williamson estate." Supposedly, "Mrs. Williamson had lost her reason," and finally, "The courts decided that Williamson was dead, and his estate was distributed according to law."

The "Lang" legend and Bierce's short story are obviously quite similar. In his book, *Among the Missing,* Jay Robert Nash debunks the old Lang tale but asserts that Bierce's story is true. As he claims:

> Over the years, a thorough investigation on the part of the author and his staff revealed, Williamson's name and place of residence have been changed for various reasons by several writers. This began when a wandering salesman named McHatten from Cincinnati was trapped by a snowstorm in 1889 in Gallatin, Tennessee. With nothing to do except drink, McHatten sat in the Sindle House Hotel and rewrote the Williamson story in an attempt to make a bit of extra change by selling it as an original report. He changed Orion Williamson's name to David Lang, the site of his disappearance from Selma, Alabama, to Gallatin, Tennessee, and the date of the occurrence from July 1854 to September 1880.[20]

Nash adds, however, that "Orion Williamson was no figment of the imagination but a real, live resident of Selma, Alabama—until, of course, he slipped into eternal mystery." While maintaining that "Orion Williamson" actually existed and that the "basic facts" of the story were true, Nash admits that "Ambrose Bierce thought the whole thing farcical and wrote a satire about the odd happening. . . ."[21]

Bierce did indeed give farcical treatment to his tales of "mysterious disappearances." Following his little trilogy is a postscript, "Science to the Front," in which he relates the theories of one "Dr. Hern, of Leipsic," alleged author of a book entitled *Verschwinden und Seine Theorie,* and an obvious crackpot. Hern postulates, says Bierce, that "in the visible world there are void places" which are likened to the "cells in a Swiss cheese." Somehow, these are supposedly the cause of such mysterious disappearances as those of Ashmore and Williamson. Bierce seems to have his tongue firmly in cheek. A search of standard reference sources including biographical dictionaries (particularly German ones), together with a bibliographic search, failed to substantiate either the existence of "Dr. Hern" or his supposed treatise.

Yet somehow Nash has discovered first names for the Bierce characters: "Orion Williamson" and "Dr. Maximilian Hern . . . author of *Disappearance and Theory Thereof.*" In response to Nash's book, some researchers suggested that further investigation should be made and— on a hint from one—I undertook the job.

Aiding me in my research were the following: Milo B. Howard, Jr., Director, State of Alabama Department of Archives and History; the Court Clerk of Dallas County, Alabama; and Eleanor R. Falkenberry, Assistant Librarian of the Public Library of Selma and Dallas County. Their searches of the 1850 and 1860 censuses, various compendiums of Alabama records, local deeds, and other sources failed to document the existence of either "Orion Williamson" or "Armour Wren."[22] Mr. Nash failed to reply to my challenge that he either prove his claims or at least clarify how he obtained his information.

The use of the unusual first name "Orion" is instructive (particularly since in Hebrew it is equivalent to "fool"[23]), and brings to mind the mythological figure who was either (1) transformed into a constellation; or (2) stung by a scorpion, which caused him to sink into the ground from whence he came.[24] In any case, the name seems fitting for a character in a hoax disappearance yarn.

The David Lang story contains a striking motif lacking in Bierce's story—that of the circle of stunted grass. (In some versions the opposite effect was reported, namely that the grass "had grown high and thick in a circle 20 feet in diameter."[25]) This seems to be a rather obvious depiction of a "fairy ring." In fairy lore, the little creatures held the power of invisibility. Futhermore,

> Those who visited fairyland, voluntarily or otherwise, usually had cause
> to regret it. In some stories, the visitor returns with scattered wits or

drained vitality and dies soon afterward; in others, he finds that many earthly years have elapsed during what seemed only a short absence, so that all his friends are dead, his home in other hands and his own name barely remembered as that of one who disappeared long ago. If he eats food while in the enchanted region, he may never escape from it at all.[26]

Fairies, we learn, "lived in subterranean palaces reached through caves or through gates magically opening in green hillsides."[27] Thus it is that "Sarah Lang" claimed that neighbors had searched the pasture carefully for some indication that her father might have fallen into a cavern. That detail—along with the fairy ring and the mysterious voice (similar to that in Bierce's "Ashmore" story and implying that Lang was in some other dimension)—alludes to fairy lore. So does the surname Lang (whether intentional or not), which recalls Andrew Lang (1844-1912), the folklorist, best known for his collections of fairy tales.

Robert Schadewald suggests that both the "Lerch" and "Lang" strains of these disappearance yarns predated Bierce; specifically that Bierce had read them, believed them, and used them as the basis for his stories.[28] But that seems unlikely.

There is no compelling evidence to indicate that "Lerch" predates Bierce. In fact, all we presently know of the earliest version of "Lerch" comes from Wilkins's booklet in which he cites a letter of March 25, 1932, from Rudolf H. Horst. Horst, then managing editor of the *South Bend Tribune,* stated that "the incident which you refer to as having occurred here in the Christmas of 1900, was purely imaginary."[29] The 1900 date for the alleged disappearance indicates (unless we postulate an Ur-"Lerch" with an earlier date) that the story was written after 1900 (and therefore well after Bierce). True, other versions give earlier dates (1889, 1890) but these were written much later and must be distrusted.

At this writing, it is difficult to narrow down the time period for the writing of the "original" Lerch story. But in any event, relying solely on the evidence at hand, it seems probable that the Lerch story is a derivation of Bierce's "Charles Ashmore's Trail," rather than vice versa.

The origin of the Lang tale is somewhat more problematical. In submitting his article to *Fate,* Stuart Palmer asserted that an earlier version of the story appeared "years ago" in an obscure magazine called *Ghost* (published during 1936-37).[30]

As noted earlier, Nash attributes the Lang yarn to one "McHatten from Cincinnati," whereas Schadewald, citing librarian Payne, gives the name as "Joe Mulhatten." Tennessee legend (possibly of recent vintage) holds that he was a traveling salesman, notorious liar, and journalistic hoaxer of the 1880s;[31] but no proof has yet been found to substantiate the assertion that the "Lang" story was actually written by "McHatten" or "Mulhatten." Such assertions cannot be accepted uncritically. In fact, "Joe Mulhatten" must surely be a corruption of "Joseph M. Mulholland, a traveling salesman of Washington, Pennsylvania, who wrote under the pseudonym of Orange Blossom in the 1880s and '90s and read his semiplausible yarns in many a serious publication, principally the *Philadelphia Public Ledger.*"[32]

Still, Mulhatten/Mulholland may have originated the basic Lang story; but if so, his original story has not surfaced. Taking the story *as we have it,* there are indications that it is later than Bierce. For instance, it is highly unlikely that Bierce would have omitted such a memorable motif as that of the fairy ring (one that is in every known Lang account) had it been in some version which inspired his own story. Furthermore, we should have to assume that Bierce changed "Lang" to "Williamson" but that later writers somehow repeatedly bypassed the well-known Bierce story and tapped the supposed earlier Lang version—a version that is so obscure (if it exists at all) that it has eluded the rest of us. Some of the same arguments apply to the "Lerch" yarn as well. If, as the evidence suggests, Bierce's "Ashmore" story—with the motif of the mysterious voice—predates "Lerch," isn't it likely that the similar motif in "Lang" derived from "Ashmore," rather than vice versa? If Bierce really took the voice motif from an earlier "Lang" version, then why is that motif in his "Ashmore" story rather than in his "Williamson" one where it would be expected—if "Williamson" were indeed derived from "Lang"?

Other factors render it doubtful that Bierce plagiarized earlier tales, much less that he believed such tales to be true. As he insisted: "Narrative fiction, intended as fiction, should seldom be based upon actual occurrences. Facts interfere with imagination, and imagination surpasses fact, and is the truer."[33]

Unless we are to presume that there are "true" accounts behind other Bierce tales, why should we assume that there are behind two of his stories? Bierce was eminently capable of devising his own plots and shaping his own tales. As his biographer, Walter Neale, states,

". . . Many is the yarn that he spun . . . the romance being told with so great fidelity to circumstance and so great verisimilitude that his hearers never doubted the actuality of the professed occurrence."[34]

All this is not to say that Bierce originated the genre of "mysterious disappearances"—or "Fortean disappearances," as they are now usually called (after Charles Fort, who loved to taunt orthodox scientists with reports of mysterious occurrences they could not explain).[35] The genre is, in fact, ancient. For example, Hebrews 11:5 reads, ". . . Enoch . . .was not found, because God had translated him. . . ." And at the end of Sophocles' play, *Oedipus at Colonus* (fifth century B.C.), Oedipus mysteriously vanishes. Then there is the 1807 case of Benjamin Bathurst who was a very real person. Bathurst did disappear under mysterious circumstances; but since he was a diplomat on a mission, carrying dispatches, he was presumed assassinated. As might be expected, one version of the case is of the Fortean variety.[36]

Bierce may have seen *Footfalls on the Boundary of Another World* (1869), written by the American diplomat Robert Dale Owen, which relates a number of spontaneous vanishings. For example, in 1802 an Irish clergyman was on his garden walk in "bright moonlight" when he saw his wife "in her usual dress" and approached her. However, she would not reply to him. Instead she passed behind some tall rows of peas; but, says Owen, when the husband "reached the open space beyond the peas the figure was nowhere to be seen. As there was no spot where, in so short a time, it could have sought concealment, the husband concluded that it was an apparition. . . ." He then found his wife in bed, seriously ill, and she soon died.[37]

Although such legends dealt with presumed "apparitions" and not actual persons, that scarcely argues against their having served as forerunners of Ambrose Bierce's "mysterious disappearance" stories. In fact, in other respects they are virtually from the same mold. Bierce was seemingly fascinated with such tales. E. F. Bleiler states that "in his old age, he collected stories of disappearances, especially those with adumbrations of the supernatural."[38]

Ambrose Bierce may have even been aware that his own name was virtually a synonym for disappearance. According to the *Oxford English Dictionary,* one meaning of *ambrose* is that it is equivalent to *ambrosia;* and the *Encyclopedia of Superstitions, Foklore and the Occult Sciences* contains this entry:

DISAPPEARANCE—In many countries if a person disappears and cannot be found, he is supposed to have eaten ambrosia and been turned by it into a fairy.[39]

It is interesting to speculate that Bierce's fascination with disappearance stories inspired him to plan his own mysterious disappearance—in late 1913 or early the next year. Walter Neale, Bierce's biographer and friend, discredits the legend that the aging Bierce died while serving with Pancho Villa in Mexico. According to Neale, Bierce had often vowed to commit suicide rather than suffer the increasing debilities of old age. To this end, he had purchased a German pistol and, says Neale, "Somewhere in the Gorge of the Colorado," he "selected the place of his last earthly habitat." Neale adds that this was in the summer of 1912 and that Bierce showed him a photo of the actual location. He "pointed out that there he would be protected from vultures."[40] To another, Bierce had vowed, "And nobody will find my bones."[41] Indeed, no one has.[42]

Select Bibliography

Bierce, Ambrose. "Mysterious Disappearances." In *Can Such Things Be?* 1893. Reprint. New York: Albert & Charles Boni, 1924. A trilogy of short stories, two of which obviously served as models for the "Lerch" and "Lang" disappearance tales.

Edwards, Frank. *Strangest of All,* 102-103. New York: Signet, 1962. An account of the fictitious tale of the disappearance of Oliver Larch, presented as a true story science cannot explain.

Nash, Jay Robert. *Among the Missing.* New York: Simon & Schuster, 1978. A book that relates—among other disappearance stories—some of the Fortean variety; debunks the "Lang" tale but wrongly asserts that Bierce's story of the vanishing of a "planter named Williamson" is true.

Schadewald, Robert. "David Lang Vanishes . . . FOREVER." *Fate,* December 1977, 54-60. An excellent exposé of the "Lang" hoax.

———." Fortean Fakes and Folklore." *Pursuit* 11, no. 3 (Summer 1978): 98-100. A debunking of "Fortean" tales of disappearance.

Wilkins, Harold T. *Mysterious Disappearances of Men and Women in the U.S.A., Britain and Europe,* 4-5. Girard, Kans.: Haldeman-Julius Publications, 1948. An early reference to the "Oliver Lerch" (tracks-in-snow) story, showing that it existed prior to 1932.

Acknowledgments

In substantially this form, this chapter appeared as "Ambrose Bierce and those 'Mysterious Disappearance' Legends," in *Indiana Folklore* (vol. 13, nos. 1-2, 1980). Thanks are extended to the editor, Linda Degh, for her assistance and for permission to reprint it.

Further thanks are due the many librarians, archivists, clerks, and others—especially those named in the text—who took the time to search records on my behalf and to provide essential information.

6. DOUBLE TROUBLE
Synchronicity and the Two Will Wests

A coincidence! . . . The odds are enormous against its being coincidence. No figures could express them. No, my dear Watson, the two events are connected—must be connected. It is for us to find the connection.

—SHERLOCK HOLMES
"The Adventure of the Second Stain"

"Believe it or not," Robert Ripley would say, but on the same day in 1981, in the maternity ward of the same hospital in Louisville, Kentucky, two women—each named Debbie Hoskins—gave birth to boys. It was the first child for each, and there were other similarities: Both women had dark blond hair; both had the same doctor; and—according to the local newspaper—both were to "turn 25 within five days of each other" later that same month.[1]

To explain such "meaningful coincidences" (conjunctions of events that seem imbued with mystical significance), psychologist Carl Jung theorized that—in addition to the usual cause-and-effect relationship of events—there was an "acausal connecting principle" which he termed *synchronicity*.[2] As he wrote:

When for instance I am faced with the fact that my tram ticket bears the same number as the theatre ticket which I buy immediately afterwards, and I receive that same evening a telephone call during which the same number is mentioned again as a telephone number, then a causal connection between these events seems to me improbable in the extreme, although it is obvious that each must have its own causality.[3]

However, Gustave Jahoda, in his *The Psychology of Superstition,* suggests that there may often be cause-and-effect relationships of which we are simply unaware.[4] In fact, Professor C. E. M. Hansel (author of *ESP: A Scientific Evaluation*) once accidentally discovered a common link in a pair of events that would otherwise have seemed completely unrelated and quite astonishing.[5]

In instances where there may be no latent causal connections, other factors could apply, among them the problem of overestimating how rare the occurrence actually is. Nobel prize-winning physicist Luis Alvarez told how, while reading a newspaper, he came across a phrase that triggered certain associations and left him thinking of a long-forgotten youthful acquaintance; minutes afterward, he came across that person's obituary. On reflection, however, Alvarez assessed the factors involved and worked out a formula to determine just how unlikely such an event would actually be. He concluded that 3,000 similar experiences could be expected every year in the United States, or approximately 10 per day.[6] Synchronous events involving family and friends would be proportionately more common.

A related problem is what psychologist Ruma Falk terms "a selection fallacy"—that occurs with anecdotal events as contrasted with scientifically selected ones. As he explains: "Instead of starting by drawing a random sample and then testing for the occurrence of a rare event, we select rare events that happened and find ourselves marveling at their non-randomness. This is like the archer who first shoots an arrow and then draws the target circle around it."[7]

Such problems should be kept in mind when confronting cases of synchronicity cited by proponents. For example, "psychic" Alan Vaughan, author of *Incredible Coincidence* (1979), reported in *Fate* magazine three instances of persons of the same name receiving identical Social Security numbers. In one of the occurrences, the two individuals even shared the same birth date.[8]

Vaughan says nothing about the possibility that one person could have been assigned the number of another *because* of the similarity of names, either by human assumption or subsequent computer error. In any event, such occurrences do not seem impressive given the many millions of persons and numbers actually involved; the frequency of such cases may be about as rare as probability would allow.

Sometimes coincidences seem so incredible that they demand serious and extended research. Such was a case I investigated a few years ago. Involving the most remarkable resemblance of two apparently unrelated persons on record, it has been termed "one of the strangest coincidences in all history."[9]

On May 1, 1903, a new prisoner, a young black man named Will West, was admitted to the federal penitentiary at Leavenworth, Kansas. At that time, fingerprinting was yet to be implemented in the United States. Identification was instead made by what was called *bertillonage* or, more commonly, the "Bertillon method of identification" (after its founder, Alphonse Bertillon). This consisted of tabulating a complicated series of body measurements and recording such other physical characteristics as eye color, scars, and so on. A photograph was also included.

While Will West was being processed, a clerk recognized him as a former inmate. "You've been here before," he remarked. "No sir," Will West replied, insisting that this was his first time at Leavenworth.

Unconvinced, the clerk searched the files. "William West," read one card. It bore measurements virtually identical with those of the new prisoner. And finally there were the photographs: It was obviously the same man.

"That looks like me, all right," Will West conceded. But he continued to protest that it could *not* be him since he had no prior arrests.

At this point prison officials realized that—according to the records— William West was a "lifer," sentenced for murder and supposedly still within the prison walls. Had he been released without the fact being noted on the card? Worse, had he escaped? Or was he just pulling a stunt, pretending to be a new prisoner in order to avoid work for a while?

A check was immediately made, and in a short time two men— William West and Will West—stood together in the same room. The effect was astounding. They were so similar that only their fingerprints could clearly distingish them. Yet according to the published accounts, the two "were unrelated."[10] At least they were not *known* to have been related (see Figure 10).

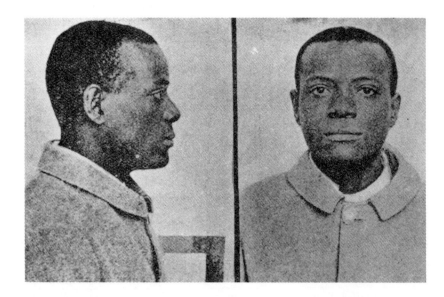

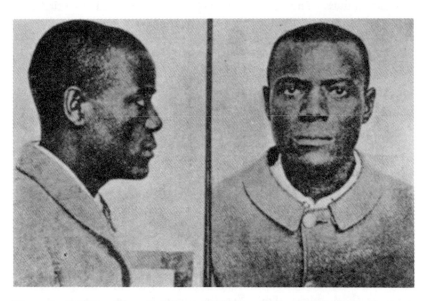

Figure 10. Full-face and profile photos of Will West (top) and William West (bottom). The uncanny resemblance of these reportedly unrelated men led to the triumph of fingerprinting over the Bertillon system of identification in America.

That is the story, albeit there are minor variations in the details. For example, while Will West was being processed, was William West "at work in one of the prison factories," or "at that minute in a Leavenworth cell"? Again, did Will West really state, "That's my picture" rather than "That looks like me"? Or did he say, as a British author phrased it, "That's my picture right enough. . . ."?[11]

The humor of Will West speaking like a Briton aside, the case was of serious consequence, for it marked the beginning of the end for *bertillonage* and a triumph for the fledgling science of fingerprinting. Yet a nagging question remained: Were the two men actually unrelated?

There *have* been cases of remarkable resemblance. For example, in 1896 and again in 1904, in London, one Adolph Beck was mistakenly identified as the swindler William Thomas and sent to prison. Only Thomas's arrest and proper identification kept Beck from serving out the second term. But although the men bore a strong general resemblance, their actual facial features—subtracting their walrus mustaches—were not really so similar. And their names, of course, were completely different.[12]

The Wests were another matter. Their uncanny resemblance was coupled with a "unique series of coincidences" to say the least, including the "accident of name."[13] The odds were being multiplied: similar facial structure *times* similar measurements *times* the same surname *times* similar first names. . . .

Since the Wests were reportedly "identical" and indeed "as alike as twin brothers,"[14] might it not be—given the absence of proof otherwise—that they *were* twins, possibly separated in early life? Would not that theory account for all the known data? The question haunted me for years. Finally I decided that—although three-quarters of a century had elapsed—I would reopen the case of "the two Will Wests." One of my first queries was to the FBI.

Inspector Homer A. Boynton, Jr., of the FBI's Public Affairs Office, wrote: "In response to your request for copies of the Wests' fingerprints, their original fingerprint cards are not on file in the FBI Identification Division. FBI policy dictates that fingerprint cards not be maintained after the eightieth birthday of the subject."[15]

Nevertheless, Inspector Boynton was able to send copies (kept by the FBI for historic purposes), which in turn were analyzed by two experts in twins' fingerprints. They were Jean Milner of the Toronto Twin Register and Dr. Margaret Thompson, a geneticist (both of the University of

Toronto). Because of the poor quality of the copies, there was a difficulty in making some of the pattern determinations, and one type of analysis could only be approximated.

Nevertheless, Dr. Thompson independently confirmed Mrs. Milner's determinations. In an overall assessment—considering the fingerprint similarities, multiplied by additional factors (same sex, similar measurements, etc.)—Mrs. Milner stated that she believed that the evidence placed the likelihood of the Wests being monozygotic twins "at a level that would be hard to dispute."[16]

Later, another fingerprint expert did dispute a few of the precise pattern determinations, and criticized certain analytical assumptions, but even he felt the total fingerprint evidence "does buttress and collaborate the relationship of the West inmates"[17] (see Figure 11).

The opinion of an expert in a uniquely different field of identification was next sought. He is Alfred V. Iannarelli, pioneer of the system of ear identification bearing his name, and internationally known for his specialized work.

Consulted in such famous questions of identification as those of Anastasia, Martin Borman, Lindbergh, and many others (including some which he is "not at liberty to state"), Iannarelli readily responded to my query. He wrote that he would be happy to assist in the West case, which he termed "indeed an interesting one."

I sent him enlarged photos of Will and William West. He in turn further enlarged the right ear of each (from the profiles), superimposing certain horizontal, vertical, and diagonal axes employed in his system of classification. Iannarelli concluded, "Your theory that [the Wests] were identical twins . . . is certainly correct. . . . I will say without a doubt, that the so-called 'West Brothers' in my opinion were related and identical twins."[18]

He enclosed "Standard Ear ID Cards with the ear photographs of both Wests" to "illustrate the anatomical classification of their ears in relation to each other." The classifications are:

Will West	M	1	3	5	0	8	6
	N	1	3	4	0	5	5
		(2)					
William West	M	1	2	5	2	8	7
	N	2	4	4	0	6	5

Figure 11. Fingerprints of the right thumbs of Will West (top) and William West (bottom) show similar "double-loop" whorl patterns (a type known to be inheritable). (Photos courtesy of the Federal Bureau of Investigation)

But abstract numerical classifications are by no means intended to replace the visual evidence itself. Iannarelli sent me several reproductions of the ears of identical and fraternal twins and triplets for comparison. It was easy to see that—although "identical" siblings did not have precisely identical ears (the classifications were different in each case)—they were markedly more alike than those termed "fraternal." The West ears possess—as Iannarelli has noted—the same exceedingly great degree of similarity as those of identical twins or any two identical triplets.

Iannarelli called attention to "the minute differences in the upper helix rim and anti-helix of Will compared to William. This of course may have taken place soon after the ears began to form during the embryological development stage. If through the classification of the external ear or fingerprints the classifications were identical, then neither system would be infallible."[19]

The Bertillon measurements and *portrait parlés* in the Wests' files— the very data that had failed to adequately distinguish the two—remained as potentially valuable evidence in the new quest to determine their relationship. The photographs, with the right ears clearly shown, had already proved extremely important.

For an opinion on the similarity of the Wests' facial features, I contacted S./Sgt. P. J. Dunleavy of the R.C.M.P. An expert with more than twenty years' experience in fingerprinting, identification photography, physical matching, and composite drawings from descriptions, Sgt. Dunleavy is also the developer of the famous Identi-Kit (Model II), which is distributed worldwide.

He commented briefly on the similarity of the Wests' fingerprint pattern types as indicating probable family relationship, and then described their facial resemblance:

> The Wests in composite artist parlance would be what we, in the profession, call "look alikes." One of the last questions I put to a witness when obtaining a composite likeness is: "Does the person being described look like anyone we would all know?"—i.e., a film star, politician, athlete, local celebrity, etc., etc. The Wests are very good examples of near perfect look alikes. They are to all intents and purposes practically indistinguishable.[20]

To draw a conclusion from Sgt. Dunleavy's expert and objective opinion, the likeness is *consistent with* their being identical twins.

I next turned to the specific Bertillon measurements from the Wests' files (see Table 1). As will be readily seen, the measurements—while extremely close—are not *exactly* the same, as has sometimes been reported by enthusiastic writers. For an evaluation of just how close the measurements were, I contacted an expert in the study of anthropometric measurements of twins, Dr. Steven Vandenberg, professor of biopsychology, Institute for Behavioral Genetics, University of Colorado. Dr. Vandenberg wrote: "The measurements you sent me for the two men are certainly consistent with the possibility that the men are twins. The small differences are well within the measurement error or could be due to real—but small—environmentally caused variations."[21]

I was unable to locate original records of the Wests' trials, or of William's pardon, or death certificates of either. (As to the latter, no records were found in Kansas or Oklahoma or Arkansas; however, the lack of a specific date and place of death made searching extremely difficult and it is entirely possible that one or both of the Wests died in one of those states.)

The FBI provided copies of the Wests' prison records, consisting of typewritten abstracts from the original files (which are no longer available at Leavenworth) and bearing stamped identification numbers 98665 through 98671.

TABLE 1
Bertillon Measurements of William and Will West

	William West[a]	Will West[b]
Height	1.77.5 (5'10")	1.78.5 (5'10½")
Outstretched Arms	1.88.0	1.87.0
Trunk	91.3	91.3
Head Length	19.8	19.7
Head Width	15.9	15.8
Cheek Width	14.8	14.8
Right Ear	6.5 (or 6.6)[c]	6.6
Left Foot	27.5	28.2
Left Middle Finger	12.2	12.3
Left Little Finger	9.6	9.7
Left Forearm	50.3	50.2

[a] Register No. 2626.
[b] Register No. 3426.
[c] Conflicting data from prison records.

These documents, containing data on the dispensation of the Wests' sentences, their Bertillon measurements, and other information, were a collective goldmine. They contained many surprises, including the fact that Will West *had* served a previous sentence at Leavenworth—under the alias "Johnson Williams." (This proves to be an important revelation as we shall see later.)

Data from the files yielded strong evidence for the twin theory. Consider this portion of document 98667: "In the file of William West, No. 2626, is the following statement: 'June 15, 1907—George Bean, No. 3662, stated to me today that he knew William West No. 2626 and also Will West No. 3426 at his home, in the territory, and that they were twin brothers. These two prisoners have acknowledged that they were distantly related, but deny that they are members of the same family. SIGNED: J. McClaughry, Acting Record Clerk.' "

So much for their being unrelated! On the contrary, despite their denials, the deposition is persuasive evidence of their being "twin brothers"; for what motive could their fellow prisoner have for lying in the matter?

Document 98668 is a bombshell. It provides the names, addresses, and *relationship to the prisoner* of persons with whom Will and William corresponded. (Actually, unless they learned in prison, neither could read or write; obviously others may have written and read for them.) The lists are somewhat long, contain no dates, and not all names are on both lists. However, *both* corresponded with a brother, John West; with sisters named Lula Harris, Emma West (she was a "Mrs." and may have been a sister-in-law), Julia Jones (and Julia Williams: Had one sister married twice?), and Mathilda (or Matilda) Johnson; and both corresponded with an uncle named George (or George J.) West! It would seem that not only were the two Wests more than "distantly related"— being in fact from the same immediate family—but that they knew it!

William's correspondence record also lists a "Will West" (at two addresses in Oklahoma: Wynona, and Strand) and "Bill West" (also at two addresses: Salisaw, Okla., and Fort Smith, Ark.). These four entries are marked by an asterisk with the notation, "Quite likely the same person." Indeed, probably this person was *the* Will West, since Will's sentence for manslaughter expired in 1909—ten years before William's release. (William was paroled August 30, 1919. This occurred despite an escape "as trusty from Outside Lawn Detail" on October 22, 1916, which resulted in his apprehension in Topeka the next day.

He eventually received a "full and unconditional pardon" on February 21, 1927.)

Will's correspondence record lists his wife as "Nellie West, Muldrow, I. T. (Okla.)." She is surely the same wife, "Nettie? Nellie," in the record of "Johnson Williams" (Will West). The "Williams" correspondence record lists "cousins" named "Andrew Williams, Lena Williams, and J. Williams." (The latter may be the Julia Williams in the records of both Wests.) Also on the "Johnson Williams" list, Will's father is given as "J. Williams." (Obviously either the name or relationship is fictitious.) As Will West, there is no record of his father; but there is for William West: He is listed as "Bose West, Tuskahoma, I.T."

Document 98665, in part, provides background information on the pair (given in Table 2 as recorded). Again, these "coincidences" are fully consistent with the hypothesis that Will and William are from the same immediate family. Both were born in Texas; both had a mother who was born in Texas and who had died before their arrests; both had moved to the Indian Territory. . . .

One apparent discrepancy is found in document 98670. The document (containing their Bertillon measurements and descriptions) gives William's age (in 1901, apparently) as twenty-one. Yet Will's age (presumably only two years later) is listed as twenty-six. The matter is resolved, however, by the file of "Johnson Williams" who, in 1897, was seventeen. Thus it seems probable that Will and William were both born in 1880.

TABLE 2
Background Information on William and Will West

	William West[a]	Will West[b]
Born	Texas	Texas
Left home	Age 13	Age 12
Education	Cannot read or write	Cannot read or write
Occupation	Miner	Farmer
Religion	Baptist	None
Usual residence	Tuskahoma, I.T. (Okla.)	Catoosa, I.T. (Okla.)
Father born	Place unknown	Texas
Mother born	Texas (deceased when received)	Texas (deceased when received)

[a] Register No. 2626.
[b] Register No. 3426.

I had hopes of locating the pair (at age ten) on the 1890 census of Texas or Oklahoma, but virtually the entire U.S. census for that year was destroyed by fire.

A professional genealogist, James M. Puckett of Atlanta, searched the Texas census index of 1880 but found no listing for "Bose West." In the records of Walker County, Texas, he did locate a pair of male Negro twins named West. One was even named "William." But the other was "John," and their ages were given as ten—a decade older than the "two Will Wests," who should then have been infants (if in fact they were born by the time the census was taken). Mr. Puckett observed that "as a person born in the South and familiar with the Black race in general, one must consider that in 1880 in the vast expanse of Texas, many were not enumerated and names meant very little, being changed practically at will."[22] Doubtless William West, or his brother Will West— a.k.a. Bill West, alias Johnson Williams—would have agreed!

In summary, we have this data as evidence that the Wests were twins: The fingerprint evidence (including similar, inheritable pattern types on corresponding fingers); the virtually identical ears; the series of extremely close anthropometric measurements; the same ages; the "look alike" facial features; the matching backgrounds (born in Texas, mother deceased, moved to Indian Territory, etc.); the statement of their fellow prisoner that he *knew* them to be twins; the correspondence records (showing that they wrote to the same brother, same sisters, and the same uncle); plus the identical last names and comparable first names.

Weighed against their claim that they were only "distantly related," the evidence is overwhelming that William West and Will West were monozygotic—identical—twins. And every indication is that they knew this to be so.

Why the deception? Perhaps in their criminal activities, one twin provided the alibi for another, or perhaps—like twins everywhere—they couldn't resist playing pranks with their resemblance. As they became the focus of increasing attention, it became difficult for them to confess the truth. Thus, when challenged that they *were* twins, they tardily admitted (just so much as might stall further inquiry) that they were "distantly related." (Interestingly, an incident transpired in 1984 in which a death-row inmate swapped places with his identical twin, who was also a prisoner at the Nebraska state penitentiary. Whether the switch was part of an escape attempt, or merely a prank, was not learned.[23])

Whatever the actual facts of the matter, one incredible detail remains to be considered. On September 7, 1901, when *William* West was first admitted to Leavenworth, *Will* West (as "Johnson Williams") was then serving out his term for embezzlement! In other words, the celebrated incident of 1903, in which one West was admitted while the other was already serving a term, was but a replay of 1901—except that in the earlier instance the amazing resemblance was *not* noted!

Or was it? Surely the two looked just as much alike then as two years later. When William was admitted, and in the 110 days before "Johnson Williams" was released (Christmas Day, 1901), how was it that their remarkable resemblance wasn't noted? Did it really take the more blatant similarity of names, in 1903, to make the difference?

Adding additional elements to the scenario provides a possible answer. In 1901 *bertillonage* held sway, and officials would necessarily have been reluctant to publicize a case so clearly demonstrating its limitations. (If the resemblance *was* noted, officials could reassure themselves that the names were different and that the measurements were not a perfect match; and they could conclude that the coincidences were only that, and therefore unlikely to be repeated.)

But in 1903, it was a different situation. In that year, according to Eugene Block, "Prison officials [in New York state] began to take the prints of their inmates as did federal penitentiaries, but many law enforcement officials continued to regard the practice as nothing more than a foolish fad."[24]

The scoffers were soon silenced by the incident at Leavenworth. Because of the West case, Leavenworth was authorized by the Department of Justice to "expend a sum not to exceed $60" for installing the fingerprint system.[25] This appears to have occurred in 1904[26] although one source states that the penitentiary went over to the new system "the very next day."[27]

All this aside, the importance of the West case remains—for its unique place in the history of identification, and for the part it played in advancing the science of fingerprinting. The case should also serve as a reminder that when "coincidences" seem too remarkable to be true, investigation—rather than invocation of mystical forces—may be in order.

Select Bibliography

Blassingame, Wyatt. *Science Catches the Criminal,* 12-13. New York: Dodd, Mead, 1975, A concise presentation of the case of the "Two Will Wests" as an incredible coincidence.

Falk, Ruma. "On Coincidences." *Skeptical Inquirer* 6, no. 2 (Winter 1981-82): 18-31. A psychologist's skeptical discussion of synchronicity, exposing some of the ill-founded assumptions of its proponents.

Hansel, C. E. M. *ESP: A Scientific Evaluation,* 193ff. New York: Scribner, 1966. A brief discussion of synchronicity in the context of a larger skeptical work on alleged extrasensory perception.

Jahoda, Gustav. *The Psychology of Superstition.* Baltimore: Penguin, 1970. A skeptical discussion of Jung's ideas on coincidence.

Jung, C. G. "Synchronicity: An Acausal Connecting Principle." In *The Collected Works of C. G. Jung,* ed. Sir Herbert Read et al. Bolligen Series, no. 20. New York: Pantheon, 1960. Jung's original treatise on "synchronicity."

Vaughan, Alan. *Incredible Coincidence.* Philadelphia: Lippincott, 1979. A credulous, popular book on synchronicity by a supposed "psychic." Contains numerous anecdotal accounts.

Acknowledgments

The featured case in this chapter was originally published as "The Two 'Will Wests': A New Verdict," in the *Journal of Police Science and Administration,* Vol. 8, No. 4 (December 1980), pp. 406-413: reprinted (in revised form) by permission of the International Association of Chiefs of Police, P.O. Box 6010, 13 Firstfield Road, Gaithersburg, Maryland 20878.

The author is grateful to the individuals and institutions mentioned in the text—particularly the experts who conducted the various analyses relating to aspects of the Wests' resemblance. Special thanks are also due Robert J. Hazen, Supervisor, Fingerprint Instruction, FBI Academy, who (subsequent to publication of the original article) located and sent good photographs of the Wests' fingerprints, and who introduced the author to speak on the subject at an international forensic conference.

7. PSYCHIC PROSPECTORS
"Witching" for Hidden Gold

I think that there is a small experiment which we may try tomorrow, Watson, in order to throw some light on the matter.

—SHERLOCK HOLMES
"The Adventure of Shoscombe Old Place"

Some would question whether dowsing—a form of divination by which one attempts to locate water, hidden treasure, or the like—should be classed as "supernatural." Modern proponents suggest that the phenomenon that sets the divinatory rod or other device in motion may have a natural explanation, and skeptics are all too ready to agree, arguing that the explanation is indeed mundane. At one time, it was thought that an "occult force" was responsible,[1] and the practice was therefore condemned by Martin Luther.[2]

Indeed, divination is categorically prohibited in Deuteronomy (18:10-12), where it is associated with witchcraft:

There shall not be found among you any one that maketh his son or his daughter to pass through the fire, or that useth divination, or an observer of times, or an enchanter, or a witch. Or a charmer or a consulter with familiar spirits, or a wizard, or a necromancer. For all that do these things are an abomination unto the Lord. . . .

Nevertheless, modern dowsing enthusiasts sometimes attempt—as did William Lilly, the seventeenth-century astrologer who used "Mosaicall rods" to hunt for treasure—to link the divining rod to Moses.[3] Moses has even been dubbed "the first water witch" because he used his staff to strike a rock which then gave forth water (Num. 20:8-11).[4]

Others would equate the divining rod with the Romans' *virgula divina* or with other divinatory sticks or magic wands—no matter how different the actual methodologies or goals.[5]

It is true that many types of divination are quite ancient—palmistry, for example, as well as crystal-gazing and astrology. Other ancient forms include Kleromancy (divination by lots), Oneiromancy (by dreams), Idolomancy (by idols or images), and countless others.[6]

Nevertheless, the practice we term dowsing—also called "witching" or rhabdomancy—can be traced to the mining camps of sixteenth-century Bohemia. Georgius Agricola (in his *De re Metallica*, 1556) spoke of "the forked twig" employed there which some claimed "is of the greatest use in discovering veins" of ore. Having cut forks from hazel bushes, the practitioners held the prongs in clenched fists. As Agricola wrote:

> They then wander hither and thither at random through mountainous regions. It is said that the moment they place their feet on a vein the twig immediately turns and twists, and so by its action discloses the vein; when they move their feet again and go away from that spot the twig becomes once more immobile.[7]

The forked twig (usually of hazel, willow, or peach) has long been a mainstay of dowsing. Other items have also been used, including: a rod with a ball on the end, a flexible stick held by its ends in an arc, a horseshoe-shaped wire rod with handles, a vertical rod having a balanced cross arm, a P-shaped wire device, a single wire loop, a pair of L-shaped copper rods, a deformed coat hanger, a pair of open pliers or scissors, a Y-shaped plastic gadget, a twist of barbed wire, a circular aluminum-wire affair, and many more. Dowsers may also use stylish contraptions of their own design, often incorporating a capsule into which can be placed samples of the sought-after substance.[8] (At least one dowser used a cartridge belt to hold an array of such capsules.[9]) Manufactured rods are also available, sporting names like "Adjustable Sensitivity Detector" (manufactured in Belgium),[10] "Magnetomatic Locator" (a Florida gadget),[11] and "Aurameter."[12]

Another class of dowsing devices is the pendulum, which can take such forms as a ring or ball suspended on a string, a watch or keyring and chain, a spool on a thread, a small plumbob on its cord, a pencil or other rod (even a crowbar!) held vertically, or a bottle (into which is placed a sample of the material being sought) on a length of twine.[13] A French artist and inventor, Jean Auscher, devised a *scripto-pendule* which traced patterns on a map with India ink.[14] And commercial versions range from "magnetized pendulums" which have "new aerodynamic shapes"[15] to the plastic "sex detectors" of novelty racks.

The latter type, which sold for many decades, illustrates the dowsing phenomenon and its attendant problems. Held over a woman's hand the pendulum will swing in circles, but over a man's hand, back and forth (that is, unless the practitioner is told that a man will cause circular movements, a woman back-and-forth ones; or that the motions will be oval for one sex, figure-8 for the other; or that some other response will be manifested). Writes Martin Gardner in his *Fads and Fallacies in the Name of Science*:

> The explanation is, of course, that unconscious and invisible movements of your hand are sufficient to start the pendulum swinging in whatever manner you *expect* it to behave. A dowsing rod operates on exactly the same principle.

As Gardner clarifies:

> The unwitting translation of thoughts into muscular action is one of the most firmly established facts of psychology. In individuals particularly prone to it, it is responsible for such "occult" phenomena as the movement of a Ouija board, table tipping, and automatic writing. It is the basis of a type of mind reading known in the magic profession as "muscle reading." Someone hides a pin in a room, and the performer finds it quickly by having a spectator take hold of his hand. The spectator thinks he is being led by the magician, but actually the performer permits the *spectator to lead him* by unconscious muscular tensions. Many famous muscle readers are able to dispense with bodily contact altogether, finding the hidden object merely by observing the reactions of spectators in the room.[16]

(The "mentalist" Kreskin has often performed this feat for television audiences.)

In fact, as the Quija phenomenon was described in the original patent application: "A question is asked and *by the involuntary muscular actions of the players,* or through some other agency, the frame will commence to move across the table."[17] (Emphasis added.) That that is indeed the case can be easily demonstrated, as magician Milbourne Christopher has explained: When the board is out of sight and the alphabet scrambled, only gibberish is spelled out.[18]

Similarly, British physicist Michael Faraday concluded that the reason tables were tilting during the spiritualist craze of the 1850s was that people were pushing them. He arranged a device which—when set on a table top with the participants' fingers upon it—would register any pressure. When the subjects were permitted to see the indicator, the table failed to move; yet, when the indicator was hidden from view, pressures were again recorded, even though many were unaware that they were actually responsible.[19]

Experiments with dowsing yield similar results that indicate muscular activity is responsible for the twitching of the divining rod. By attaching a measuring instrument to the rod and then wiring one of the wrist muscles to the apparatus, a physiologist demonstrated that the rod's movement was preceded by the muscle's contraction by approximately one-half of a second.[20]

Although many dowsers still maintain that some "force" acts directly upon the rod to set it in motion, some modern proponents do not dispute the evidence to the contrary. They instead claim that the physiological reaction is the result of some as-yet-unexplained psychic stimulus such as clairvoyance (a form of ESP—literally, "clear seeing").[21]

Regardless of the cause attributed to it, dowsers report success with their eccentric "art," but Gardner observes:

> . . . If you dig deep enough, almost anywhere, you are bound to hit water. Water fairly close to the surface is far more plentiful than one might think, and the odds of finding it at shallow depth, at a spot picked at random, are in many regions very high. Actually, water seldom occurs in "veins" (except in rare cases where rock fractures or cavities permit it). There is merely a variable porosity of ground-water below a certain level, which varies from year to year and season to season.

In most areas, it is impossible to *avoid* finding ground-water, though it is seldom in sufficient quantity to supply more than a local household.[22]

According to such critics, dowsers are invariably seasoned outdoorsmen with some knowledge of the subject at hand (water wells, oil, gold, land mines in Vietnam, etc.), who may subconsciously make use of visual cues.

As the late Milbourne Christopher, former head of the Occult Investigating Committee of the Society of American Magicians, stated:

The best dowsers are people who are familiar with the soil on which they walk, or who have through experience a knowledge of how the earth appears over areas beneath which there is water.[23]

(Type and amount of vegetation can be one indicator, for example.)

In any event, despite the claims of success by dowsing enthusiasts, the "witchers" actually fare poorly in properly controlled tests of their abilities. For example, an experiment conducted under the auspices of the American Society for Physical Research in 1949 pitted twenty-seven diviners against a water engineer and a geologist. As shown by shafts sunk at the indicated points, the scientists were relatively successful in estimating depth of water at specific points, whereas the dowsers failed utterly. According to the report, "not one of our diviners could for a moment be mistaken for an 'expert.' . . . We saw nothing to challenge the prevailing view that we are dealing with unconscious muscular activity. . . ."[24]

Another test was conducted in 1964 by James A. Coleman, professor of physics at the American International College in Springfield, Massachusetts. Ten garden hoses were placed a few feet apart and covered with canvas; only one hose was attached to a water source. Professor Coleman offered a reward to any dowser who could locate the correct hose in seven out of ten attempts. Of the three who tried, two failed four times in a row each and admitted defeat. The third located the correct hose twice, then failed four times. Professor Coleman, who retained his reward money, concluded: "Dowsing is nothing but self-delusion."[25]

In 1979, several Italian diviners failed to collect a $10,000 reward offered by magician James Randi. The task was to trace the irregular course of a pipe that traversed a small plot. Four dowsers—including a Professor Lino Borga, who was "enthusiastic, effervescent, and loquacious in the extreme"—traced zig-zag paths with a variety of divining devices. Not only were they unable to divine the correct route, but two were unable even to tell whether there was water in the pipe at all.[26]

In the meantime, I had conducted my own tests of dowsers' abilities. Mine took place in the famed Klondike gold fields and involved prospectors who employed their supposed divinatory skills to locate that precious yellow metal.

At the time, I was living in Dawson City—"the heart of the Klondike"—in Canada's Yukon Territory, where my adventurous spirit had led me to briefly settle in 1975-76. During the winter I was exhibit designer for the renovated local museum with its historic gold-rush artifacts. Summers saw me working nights—with waxed moustache and costume complete with sleeve garters—dealing blackjack and operating a wheel of fortune in Diamond Tooth Gertie's Gambling Hall. Days saw me variously engaged in managing a river tour business, going hunting and prospecting (see Figure 12) and staking gold claims, and serving as a "stringer" for the *Yukon News*.[27]

It was while wearing my reportorial hat that I assembled four Dawson-area dowsers for a test of their strange craft. I thought it something of a unique opportunity, since although it is water-witching that tends to dominate dowsing, divining for gold has at least an equally long and parallel history.

Dowsing as we know it apparently began in sixteenth-century Bohemia as a means of searching for metallic ores. In the same century the Earl of Westmoreland's son was investigated for occult practices and for using a ring to locate hidden treasure; two priests, among other persons, were convicted for supposedly conjuring up spirits to help them discover the whereabouts of a chest of gold; and a Sussex laborer was pilloried for fraud for persuading the king's subjects "that by conjuration and invocation of evil spirits they might discover hidden hoards of gold and silver, and regain lost goods."[28] In the following century, John Locke was speaking of the "deusing-rod" (sic) which was "able to discover mines of gold and silver."[29]

This early practice of divining for gold and other treasure had accompanied the gold-rush stampeders to the Klondike, as recorded in archival photographs. One shows a woman in the doorway of her tent-topped structure—its sign, "FORTUNES TOLD $1," no doubt addressed to

Figure 12. The author finding gold the hard way—panning for it on Bonanza Creek in the Klondike gold fields, 1975.

the "cheechakos" (or newcomers).[30] Another photo depicts a diviner with his trusty rod, which one imagines was used in searching for the coveted indigeneous metal.[31]

I rounded up four such searchers, and assembled them on one of the famous gold-rush-era claims on Bonanza Creek. (It had belonged to Harry Leamon and was designated "No. 56 B.D."—i.e. fifty-sixth below the original or "Discovery" claim.)[32] The four, who had agreed to a controlled test of their ability, were:

- Art "Arizona" Wilks, 62, a U.S. prospector who had been visiting the Yukon on and off since 1947. He stated that he had begun dowsing "as a kid: but I didn't know what I was doing." He had since become a dedicated dowser and had a placer gold claim.
- Jerry Leverman, 50, a former Nova Scotian who had lived year-round in the Klondike since 1953. Previously a self-described "engineering assistant," he had twelve years' experience as a dowser and worked a placer claim at "Whiskey Hill" on Hunker Creek.
- Anthony "Tony" Fritz, 62, a local commercial fisherman born in Austria. He had been witching for about twenty years, and also had a placer claim.
- Richard "Captain Dick" Stevenson, 46, a former logger and territorial wolf poisoner, who ran his own river tour business. A relative amateur to the practice of dowsing, he had been taught by Leverman some four years previously, and now prospected constantly. Like the others, he had a gold claim.

Also present at the August 24, 1976, gathering at "No. 56 B.D." were the following:

- Don and Sue Murphy, owners of the historic claim (which had reportedly yielded $25 pans of the precious metal at a time when that was a small fortune). They had spent the past year digging a 180-foot hard-rock tunnel.
- Glenn Tepaske, who worked with Leverman on his "Whiskey Hill" claim.
- Randy Wilks, "Arizona's" son.

As everyone gathered for the field test, the scene was just as peculiar as one might expect: as if being tugged along by an unseen cord, the rhabdomancers traced, crossed, retraced, or paralleled each other's meandering paths, their copper or willow wands bobbing wildly or swinging in bold arcs or—in the case of double rods held parallel— swinging abruptly apart or crossing firmly over the dowser's chest. Such movements—the practitioners claimed—indicated underground deposits or veins of gold or water (see Figure 13).

Of course, as no drilling would take place, such assertions, together with allegations of previous successes—of mineral bodies pinpointed, of lost objects found, or of questions successfully answered (rod or pendulum allegedly giving the appropriate *yes* or *no* response)—would remain unproved. In fact, when I asked "Arizona" for the address of a man for whom he boasted he had recovered a lost object, he told me—rather evasively I thought—that he no longer knew the man's whereabouts. Scientists regard such unverifiable tales of past successes as mere "anecdotal evidence."

The dowsers insisted on some specific tests which—although they had methodological flaws—were permitted with the understanding that they were not to be considered part of the official examination. For example, Captain Stevenson attempted to locate the person from whom a lock of hair had been cut and affixed to his divining rod. Although it would seem that he would have had an advantage from the appearance of the hair alone, he nevertheless failed the test. His wand dipped— erroneously—over Sue Murphy's head, but she then admitted she had cut and affixed the hair. This was against Stevenson's specific instructions that the subject was to do everything himself. A second, similar test was then conducted and Stevenson once again failed to locate the correct individual.

Early in the afternoon Tony Fritz insisted he be allowed to "witch" for a hidden object using his pendulum. We were grouped near a mine shaft and Fritz walked out of sight toward the cabin while a gold watch was carefully placed under a large rock. He spent several minutes dowsing in the area, once walking right over the hiding place, but he failed to locate the watch. He insisted afterward that he had defined a triangular area around the watch, but I pointed out that that area was bordered by an embankment, a pond, and the road, and that he had simply delineated the area to which he knew the object was confined.

Figure 13. "Captain" Dick Stevenson wielding his copper dowsing rods in a search for gold on the old Leamon claim, Bonanza Creek, Yukon Territory.

At one point during his search, I had to reprimand Sue Murphy with a stern look when she blurted out to Fritz, "You're not even close!" Given the confined area, the implications of that statement could have narrowed the search by 50 percent. However, Fritz did not seem to benefit from it, or from any unconscious cuing, and his negative results would seem to have precluded his having received deliberate signals from any bystander. (I was not overly suspicious of the group, but it was clear they wanted very badly to convert "the skeptic.") Fritz's fellow dowsers rationalized his failure by claiming that the test had been conducted over a "hot spot" of gold.

At one point I had an exchange with "Arizona," whose loquaciousness and braggadocio could scarcely be ignored. He was showing me how a subterranean "hot spot" of gold caused his set of L-shaped copper rods to cross every time he passed over the spot. I pointed out that I could see his hands move slightly each time, but he insisted it was the "pull" on the ends of the rods that was *causing* his hands to move in response.

He subsequently insisted that I try the rods myself. He prompted me by pointing out the spot at which they would cross, but I was not influenced by the suggestion and the rods remained parallel. "Arizona" insisted that I try again with him at my side to transfer some of his alleged divinatory power to me. "You're pushing on my arm," I protested, as a rod moved sharply. "No I'm not," insisted the outgoing prospector.

Don Murphy defended "Arizona." Characterizing himself as a former skeptic (a rather stock claim of believers), Murphy told how "Arizona" had divined a spot on the old Leamon claim and then done a reading for depth. (For this the number of back-and-forth, or, alternately, up-and-down, movements of the rod is counted as a certain number of feet. Curiously, the mystical forces seem to operate on our English system of measurement.) When Murphy sank a shaft he got his first "colors" (flakes of gold) at the predicted depth of 17 feet. Tony Fritz did at one point sound a skeptical note when he asked (in so many words): If we're so smart, why ain't we rich?

But this commonsense question merely unleashed the bottled-up ire of the others, who spoke disparagingly of "too many skeptics" and of geologists who "resent" dowsers. According to Leverman, geology is the "easiest profession" to prepare for in college. Neither were assayers spared; they supposedly performed careless work and relied on too-limited samples. The dowsers went on to complain that it is difficult for prospectors to get backers when dowsers are known to be involved. "They'll run away like flies," asserted Leverman. "They think we're goofy."

As a group, the dowsers tended to dismiss any occult connection and instead attributed the movement of rod or pendulum to some physical—if hitherto unknown—"rays" or "waves" or "force." The dowser was seen as something of a human compass. Jerry Leverman thought the actual explanation "a lot simpler than most people think." To him, every type of material has a "dielectric constant" and he viewed the human body as analogous to a radio with the divining rod as the "antenna." He employed a copper rod, he explained, because copper is a superior conductor.

Although I was quite skeptical of such claims, I was nevertheless eager to test the subjects in hopes of witnessing some conclusive results. To my simple test the four dowsers had readily agreed.

It involved preparing a number of small, identical cardboard boxes into which was placed gold or other test material—or nothing whatsoever. Two groups of ten boxes each were decided upon. These were scrambled by mixing them in a large bag; then they were drawn out one at a time and their bottoms marked (1-10 and A-J). Thus even I would not know what any given box held, and could not inadvertently cue a test subject (as by my facial expression) when he was getting "warm." The boxes were finally sealed and brought with me to the gathering.

So as to rule out any distracting subterranean influence, I had the dowsers ply their rods in search of an area all would agree was "void." At that spot some planks were arranged end to end to provide an even surface, and the boxes were placed along them, about 18-20 inches apart. (The boxes were arranged randomly and then scrambled after each dowser's guesses were tabulated.) Glenn Tepaske agreed to assist by separately recording the guesses and thus providing a check on the accuracy.

The diviners congregated in the Murphys' log cabin on the property until each was called out in turn. Each used his favorite method—single or double rods, or pendulum—and was allowed as much time as he wanted to dowse over the row of boxes. One search in either series was conducted, curiously enough, for tobacco. (Captain Stevenson specifically requested this. I had once seen him entertain tourists on his Yukon paddlewheeler by having them hide his bag of roll-your-own tobacco, which he then attempted—unsuccessfully—to locate by dowsing.) The test subjects—"Arizona" in particular—inquired how many boxes contained either tobacco or gold, but I pointed out that that information could bias the results. In any case, I added, I did not know what was in any given group of boxes.

After the individual guesses were all recorded[33] we gathered again in the cabin to check the scores. "Arizona" jokingly leaned a rifle against the table, quipping that the results had better be favorable. The boxes were opened one at a time in everyone's presence, with Glenn and me each recording.[34] Alas, the dowsers collectively scored just three hits, but they had twenty-one misses. That is, they were wrong seven times for every time they were correct.

Even though the overall test procedure (including the use of the cardboard boxes, the spaces between them, and the location of the test) had been approved in advance by all four dowsers, all expressed criticisms *after* the poor results were learned. It was "Arizona" who later came up with the rationalization that something in the green coloration of the boxes—lead perhaps—had shielded out the "rays" emanating from the test materials. In that case, I countered, why were there so many guesses that certain boxes held test substances which in fact did not? Since all the boxes had the same imagined shielding, shouldn't the dowsing rods and pendulums have failed to respond, rather than have responded too frequently?

I was wasting my breath, of course. It was clear to me that nothing would dissuade the dowsers. They had, it seemed, been long accustomed to counting their hits and ignoring or rationalizing away their misses. The "art" had survived from at least the sixteenth century; no doubt it would persist for some time to come.

Select Bibliography

Bird, Christopher. *The Divining Hand.* New York: Dutton, 1979. A useful popular compendium of dowsing history, theory, and illustrations—albeit entirely too credulous. (For example, Bird takes seriously the spoon-bending tricks of Israeli "psychic" Uri Geller.)

Christopher, Milbourne. *ESP, Seers and Psychics: What the Occult Really Is.* New York: Crowell, 1970. A professional magician's look at the "occult," with chapters on dowsing, Ouija boards, table tilting, and related phenomena.

Gardner, Martin. *Fads and Fallacies in the Name of Science*. New York: Dover, 1957. A classic work examining eccentric theories and pseudosciences, including chapters on dowsing, ESP, and related subjects.

Randi, James. "A Controlled Test of Dowsing Abilities." *Skeptical Inquirer* 4, no. 1 (Fall 1979): 16-20. A professional magician and paranormal investigator's report on his test of Italian water dowsers (who failed the experiment).

Vogt, Evon Z., and Ray Hyman. *Water Witching U.S.A.* 2nd ed. Chicago: University of Chicago Press, 1979. A valuable skeptical examination of dowsing by an anthropologist and a psychologist.

Acknowledgments

Of those mentioned in the text who assisted in arranging the field test, I am especially grateful to "Captain" Dick Stevenson for his energetic help. I also want to express my thanks to the *Yukon News* for allowing me a generous portion of newspaper space (in the September 1, 1976, issue) for publication of my rather lengthy original report.

8. CELESTIAL PAINTING
Miraculous Image of Guadalupe

And you, a trained man of science, believe it to be supernatural?

—SHERLOCK HOLMES
The Hound of the Baskervilles

Mexico's Image of Guadalupe is a sixteenth-century depiction of Mary, the Virgin Mother of Christ in the New Testament, upon a cactus-fiber tilma (or cloak). She is dressed in a robe and mantle, her hands pressed together in prayer, and at her feet are an angel and crescent moon. According to pious legend the Virgin caused the Image to appear miraculously as a "sign" to a skeptical bishop so that he would build a shrine to her. "Yearly," according to Jody Brant Smith's *The Image of Guadalupe,* "an estimated ten million bow down before the mysterious Virgin, making the Mexico City church the most popular shrine in the Roman Catholic world next to the Vatican."[1]

So popular is the Image itself that "You will find every imaginable representation of her in the churches. . . . You may find her outlined in neon as part of a downtown spectacular, chalked into a hillside, on a throwaway advertising a mouthwash, pricked out in flowers in public parks; clowns and hucksters will distribute booklets about her as a

---

Investigated with John F. Fischer.

preliminary to hawking patent medicines. . . . Bullfighters have her image woven into their parade capes; she is a popular tattoo subject; almost everyone wears her medal." Her full title is "the Most Holy Virgin Mary, Our Lady of Guadalupe, Queen of Mexico and Empress of the Americas."[2]

In the United States is at least one monastery bearing the name "Our Lady of Guadalupe." A Catholic organization, Center for Applied Research in the Apostolate, in Washington, D.C., includes among its research goals: "to seek to establish a scientific basis for devotion to Our Lady under the title of Guadalupe."[3] Another organization, one expressly concerned with the cloth, is the Image of Guadalupe Research Project, Inc., which is conducting a "scientific" study of the Image. Perhaps not surprisingly, some of its members also serve on the Shroud of Turin Research Project, Inc., which has been promoting the authenticity of another "miraculous" cloth for the past few years. We have been following the activities of both projects, and this is the result of our investigation of the Guadalupan Image to date.

The Legend

As told in the sixteenth-century *Nican Mopohua* ("an account")—written in the native Aztec language and sometimes called the "gospel of Guadalupe"[4]—the cloth's story began in early December of 1531, some ten years after Cortez had defeated the Aztec Empire. At that time an Aztec peasant, a recent Christian convert named Juan Diego, supposedly left his own village to attend Mass in another. As he passed the foot of a hill named Tepeyac, he heard birds singing, saw a bright light atop the hill, and heard a voice calling, "Juanito."

Climbing to the hill's summit, Juan Diego came upon a young girl, radiant in a golden mist, who identified herself as "the ever-virgin Holy Mary, Mother of the True God," and said, "I wish that a temple be created here quickly, so I may therein exhibit and give all my love, compassion, help, and protection, because I am your merciful mother. . . ." She instructed the peasant to hasten to "the palace of the Bishop of Mexico," Father Juan de Zumarraga, and "say to him that I manifest my great desire, that here on this plain a temple be built to me. . . ."

Now the bishop was in his palace, attended by servants, and so the poor peasant had first to plead for an audience and then suffer a long wait before finally being ushered into the holy man's presence. On bended knee, Juan Diego relayed his message to the skeptical prelate, who then sent him away while he pondered the incredible tale.

When Juan Diego reported to the Virgin at Tepeyac, she told him to return to Father Zumarraga, who now asked Juan to bring him a "sign" so that he might believe. Unfortunately, Juan was delayed by an uncle's grave illness, and therefore, seeking a priest, attempted to bypass Tepeyac "so he could not be seen by her who sees well everywhere" (as the pious account explains). However, telling him, "Let not your heart be disturbed," the Virgin assured the Indian she had just cured his uncle. And now, although it was not the season for them, Juan was to gather flowers—which he discovered blooming miraculously— wrap them in his mantle, and carry them to the doubting priest.

Once again suffering a lengthy wait, Juan Diego was finally granted an audience before the prelate, whereupon "He then unfolded his white cloth, where he had the flowers; and when they had scattered on the floor, all the different varieties of *rosas de Castilla,* suddenly there appeared the drawing of the precious Image of the ever-virgin Holy Mary, Mother of God, in the manner as she is today kept in the temple at Tepeyac, which is named Guadalupe. When the bishop saw the image, he and all who were present fell to their knees." The bishop then placed the cloth in his private chapel "until the temple dedicated to the Queen of Tepeyac was erected where Juan Diego had seen her."[5]

One of course recognizes in the legend a number of motifs from the Old and New Testaments, not only an apparition like the biblical "apparitions of superterrestrial beings" as Luis Medina Ascensio observes,[6] but also the following: the holy personage, bathed in radiant light, upon a mountain (Matthew 17:2); a divine command for the building of a place of worship (Exodus 25:8); the sending of an emissary to persuade a doubter to carry out the divine instructions (Exodus 3:18-19); the childlike attempt to avoid the all-seeing deity (Jonah 1:3-4); a miraculous healing (Matthew 9:27–35, Luke 4:39); a miraculous blossoming (Numbers 17:8, Isaiah 35:1); and an apparition's ultimate convincing of a doubter with tangible "signs" (John 20:25-30). And when the Virgin tells Juan Diego to cease worrying about his sick uncle, she echoes Christ's words to his disciples in John 14:1.

In fact, some historians believe the Guadalupan legend was itself borrowed. The report of a formal investigation of the cloth in 1556 makes clear that the name Guadalupe had by that time been given to the Tepeyac site, and the very name arouses suspicion. Historian Jacques LaFaye calls attention to the similarity of the Mexican story to an earlier Spanish legend in which the Virgin appeared to a shepherd and led him to discover a statue of her. The Spanish site was even on a river known as Guadalupe (that is, "hidden channel"), strongly suggesting that the Mexican tale was prompted by the Spanish one.[7]

And the specific story of the Virgin's appearance to Juan Diego (as distinct from the Image and the name Guadalupe, both probably dating from circa 1531) may stem from a later period than had once been supposed. A priest had estimated that the original *Nican Mopohua* had been written between 1540 and 1545—or at least 1548, the latter supposedly marking the death of Juan Diego, who, the priest argued, had supplied the writer of the account with the information.[8] But the writer, one "Antonio Valeriano," does not say so, nor is there any evidence that Juan Diego had any contact with him. Moreover, no mention was made of either Juan Diego or the legend in the entire 1556 report.[9] Thus the *Nican Mopohua* would appear to date from after that time. (Although it was once suggested that the earliest extant text of that "gospel" was written on cactus-fiber—and therefore native—paper, actually the pages' watermarks reveal them to be European.[10]) Smith says "most scholars" now believe the original account was penned sometime between 1551 and 1561,[11] and if we amend that to "after 1556" we shall perhaps be closer to the truth.

Then there is the tradition of the miraculous portrait. Smith equates the Guadalupan Image with earlier pictures that were said to be "not made with hands" (*acheiropoietos* in the Greek).[12] We agree that the legend places the picture in this tradition, but find that this raises further doubts about its authenticity because the tradition of "not-made-with-hands" images is one of pious frauds; they range from the spurious sixth-century "self-portrait" of Christ known as the "Image of Edessa"; to its later variant, "Veronica's Veil"; to the best-known example, the infamous Shroud of Turin. (The latter's provenance can be documented no earlier than the middle of the fourteenth century, at which time a bishop reportedly uncovered the artist who confessed that the "shroud" was his handiwork. Recent tests show that the image on the Turin cloth contains artists' pigments.[13])

Even separated from the legend, the Virgin of Guadalupe is linked to another tradition of "miraculous" representations of Mary. It is of the "dark-colored, ancient Greek Madonnas," which, says Jameson, "had all along the credit of being miraculous."[14] And Smith points out that the Mexicans have dubbed the Guadalupan Image "La Morena"—that is, "the dark-complexioned woman"—because of the brownish flesh tones.[15]

Another obvious sign of legend-making is the fact that statements of specific religious dogma have been put in the mouth of the Virgin when—in the *Nican Mopohua*—she describes herself as "the ever-virgin Holy Mary." As Marcello Craveri explains in his *The Life of Jesus*:

> About the end of the fourth century, John Chrysostom proposed the definition of Mary's "perpetual virginity", since her physical intactness had not been impaired by the birth of Jesus and she had maintained her virginity to the end of her life, she was to be called *a* virgin *ante partum, in partu, post partum.* This formula was to become dogma at the Lateran Council of 649 and was to be confirmed by the Tolentino Council of 675, because not everyone had freely accepted it.

(Craveri goes on to tell how theologians who postulated Mary's "perpetual virginity" had to rationalize "the embarrassing fact that the Gospels pointed clearly to brothers and sisters of Jesus," as in Mark 6:3, by transforming them into first "stepbrothers" and "stepsisters"—children of an invented earlier marriage of Joseph—and later to "cousins" of Jesus.)[16]

Also present in the legend of the Lady's appearance to Juan Diego is *hyperdulia*—the ecclesiastical term for the special veneration given to the Virgin Mary. As Craveri points out, it was after the Council of Ephesus (in 431) that a cult of the Virgin originated, and Mary eventually "assumed the functions of divinity."[17] And so, in the legend of Juan Diego in the *Nican Mopohua*, it is the Virgin who appears to him, the Virgin who is all-seeing and able to work miraculous cures, the Virgin to whom the temple is to be built, and the Virgin whose image appears for veneration. Christ is scarcely mentioned.

To these disturbing elements in the tale—the familiar motifs; the suspiciously similar Spanish story and the transported name, Guadalupe; together with the scandalous, "not-made-with-hands" portrait tradition and the blatant elements of religious dogma—we must add still one further parallel that smacks of deliberate legend manufacture. As Smith states: "The shrine which held the Image of Guadalupe had been erected on a hill directly in front of the spot where there had been an important temple dedicated to the Aztec virgin goddess Tonantzin, 'Little Mother' of the Earth and Corn."[18] Thus—in what is difficult to ascribe to coincidence—the Christian tradition became grafted onto the Indian one (a process folklorists call syncretism). As evidence of the resulting confusion between the two, some of the Indians continued to use the name Tonantzin for the Virgin of Guadalupe.[19]

The result was that the "miracle" played a "major role" in hastening the conversion of the conquered Indians. Countless thousands came to view the Image and "In just seven years, from 1532 to 1538, eight million Indians were converted to Christianity."[20] That was certainly the desired goal, since it is well known that "The propagation of Christianity was one of the main purposes of Spanish imperialism, and church and state were closely connected."[21] And since the chief organizer of the church in Mexico was Juan de Zumarraga, who became the country's first bishop in 1528, might it not have been him who instigated what now appears to have been a pious fraud, commissioning perhaps a local artist to create a suitable picture?

The Image

Turning from folkloristics to iconography, again we find considerable borrowing. Even without knowing anything of the pious legend, one would at first sight recognize the Image as a portrait of the Virgin Mary. That recognition factor is not without considerable significance, since— as St. Augustine lamented in the fifth century—it is impossible to know what the Virgin actually looked like. We recognize her in a given painting because the likeness has been established by artistic convention.

The Image of Guadalupe is obviously a devotional (as opposed to narrative) portrait, but we can more specifically characterize the picture in terms of motifs and type. First of all, we note that the Virgin stands alone; as De Bles tells us, "Representations of the Madonna without the child were extremely rare" until the middle of the fifteenth century.[22]

Next one observes the golden rays and crescent moon—motifs taken from Revelation 12:1, which many believe refers to the Virgin: "And there appeared a great wonder in heaven; a woman clothed with the sun, and the moon under her feet, and upon her head a crown of twelve stars." Although the Image has no crown, there is evidence of repainting in the area that suggests it once was present but was painted out.[23] Also, early copies of the Image do show the Virgin with the crown motif from Revelation.[24]

Her radiance, her being "clothed with the sun" as Revelation says (or "her garments were shining like the sun," as it is given in the *Nican Mopohua*), is represented as a rayed glory or aureole, a nimbus surrounding the entire figure; that is a stock artistic device, reserved for divinity and—by the Renaissance—conventionally rendered in gold (rather than the earlier white).[25] The crescent moon is another traditional element, one especially indicative of the Virgin (since, as the moon reflects the sun, her glory is borrowed from her son, the Sun of Righteousness).[26]

Other standard artistic motifs that appear in the Image of Guadalupe are the mantle's forty-six stars, signifying the number of years required for building the temple of Jerusalem;[27] gold fleur-de-lis designs that are symbolic of the Virgin Mother;[28] an angel at the Lady's feet;[29] a decorative tassel;[30] and others, including a possible Aztec motif: a distinctive lower fold of the robe.[31]

In fact, a Spanish painting, a Virgin of Mercy by Bonanat Zaortiza (now in the Museo de Arte de Cataluna in Barcelona), is said to be "of the exact form as the Virgin of Guadalupe" and even has "a similar brooch at the throat," according to Philip Serna Callahan, who terms it "strikingly imitative of the Virgin of Guadalupe,"[32] although it preceded the latter picture by nearly a century!

All of the motifs mentioned thus far are held to be later additions, at least by pro-authenticity writers. Callahan, who made a three-hour visual inspection of the image and took a series of infrared photographs, says: "Some time after the original image was formed, the moon and the tassel were added by human hands. . . . Some time after the tassel and the moon were added, the gold and black line decorations, angel, Aztec fold of the robe, sunburst, stars and background were painted. . . ." Callahan adds, "The additions were by human hands and impart a Spanish Gothic motif to the painting."[33]

Callahan thinks that some of the supposedly later work was added "probably during the 17th century";[34] however, we believe he is in error: A copy now lodged in Europe, dating from probably fewer than forty years after the original Image turned up, is actually "identical with the original" (except for the copy's "more skillfully done" gold rays and crown); it even has the identical number of stars on the Virgin's mantle.[35]

More difficult to disprove is Smith's guess that the added details— the gold rays, stars and fleur-de-lis designs, and the moon and angel— were done "in the late sixteenth century."[36] The burden of proof is not ours but his and Callahan's, and neither is able to prove that all of the tell-tale artistic motifs were absent from the "original" image. Our argument is not with their claim that overlapping of paint demonstrates that some parts were painted later than others;[37] rather, we simply remain unconvinced that much time has necessarily elapsed between the different applications. Paintings are invariably done in stages, and so what Smith and Callahan are assuming are years between stages could be merely days or even hours.

True, if some horizontal crease marks that have caused breaks in the figure have not also marred the background, as Callahan says they have not, then he draws a reasonable conclusion when he states, ". . . we must assume that the background was added after the rest of the painting was formed."[38] It is a *reasonable* conclusion, but not the only one. Other possibilities are that the background paint was (at least at that time) more resilient and so resisted cracking, or that it was subsequently repaired.

In any case, even if some elements were indeed added later, that does little to prove that the "original" portions are therefore "inexplicable" and even "miraculous," as Callahan terms the "original figure, including the rose robe, blue mantle, hands and face."[39] The fact that those areas are less thickly painted does *not* suggest that they are not painted, let alone that they are *acheiropoietos*. Indeed Callahan concedes that the robe "may *appear* to be tempera" (though he finds it "truly inexplicable") and says of the blue mantle, "The pigment is too thickly laid on to be water color. . . ."[40] Its hue, he finds, is quite close to "Mayan" blue,[41] suggesting that it could be an indigenous pigment.

And as to the hands and face, again there is evidence of painting. Callahan's infrared photographs reveal that the hands have been modified (outlined, and some fingers shortened).[42] He sees this as another instance of someone changing the Image at a later date, whereas we point out that such modifications are common to original paintings. (In fact, evidence of reworking is often used to distinguish an original—which might bear the changes of an artist creating a new work—from a copy, which need have no changes.) And Callahan can blithely speak of "the gray and 'caked' looking white pigment of the face and hands."[43] His close-up photograph of the face[44] shows that this pigment is applied so heavily in the highlight areas (exactly where an artist would be expected to heavily apply a light-toned pigment) that it obscures the texture of the cloth. Callahan even says: "Overall, the Virgin of Guadalupe appears to be a tempera painting."[45]

In short, the very areas that Callahan and Smith cite as "original" and "miraculous" all have what "appears" to be pigment or paint. One of Callahan's major reasons for supposing that the apparent paint is not paint (at least not paint of this world!), stems from his comparing the Guadalupan Image with other Indian works done in paint on cloth. He states, "The preserved Indian Codices [or histories] are invariably in tattered condition. The colors are faded and cracked in most cases and the cloth torn and in extremely poor condition." He adds, "This is in considerable contrast to the bright coloring and excellent condition of the cloth tilma of the Virgin of Guadalupe. . . ."[46] But perhaps others can understand, if Callahan cannot, that Codices—which suffer considerable handling so that they can be read—might be in worse condition than a cloth that was carefully mounted and (as early as 1647) protected by glass, followed a few years later by a protective backing.[47]

Actually, there is obvious cracking and flaking of the Guadalupan Image all along a vertical seam that passes through the "original" areas of mantle, neck, and robe, as well as through the nonmiraculous background areas (see Figure 14). This line serves as an indicator that the entire portrait was rendered in a paint-like substance.

Nevertheless, because Callahan's infrared photography failed to reveal any preparatory sketching or underdrawing, he feels strongly that the Image was not produced by human hands.[48] Even if, for the moment, we accept his claim that there is no underdrawing in the "original" areas, that claim must be tempered by the realization that his infrared technique *also failed to reveal any undersketching even in the areas which proponents concede were painted by human hands,* namely, the angel, crescent moon, and background areas. (We might point out that, with an antique religious icon we once examined, infrared photography also failed to show sketch lines, although such lines were later revealed when we examined the icon with a model-J infrared microscope, manufactured by Research Devices, Inc. This microsoope utilizes an S-1 photocathode image converter tube which extends from 400nm to 1200nm.) Besides, by the

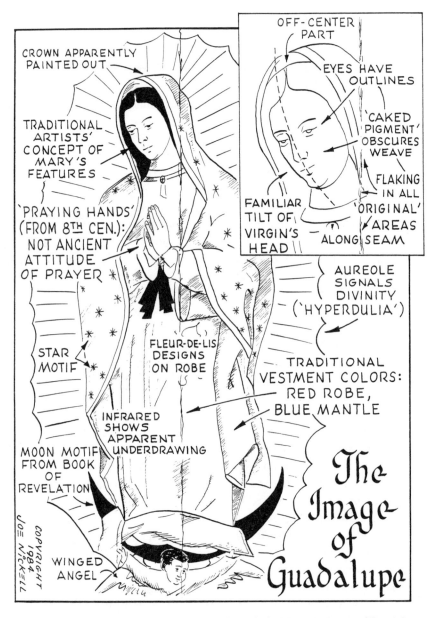

CROWN APPARENTLY PAINTED OUT

TRADITIONAL ARTISTS' CONCEPT OF MARY'S FEATURES

'PRAYING HANDS' (FROM 8TH CEN.): NOT ANCIENT ATTITUDE OF PRAYER

STAR MOTIF

MOON MOTIF FROM BOOK OF REVELATION

WINGED ANGEL

COPYRIGHT 1984 JOE NICKELL

OFF-CENTER PART

EYES HAVE OUTLINES

'CAKED PIGMENT' OBSCURES WEAVE

FLAKING IN ALL 'ORIGINAL' AREAS ALONG SEAM

FAMILIAR TILT OF VIRGIN'S HEAD

AUREOLE SIGNALS DIVINITY ('HYPERDULIA')

FLEUR-DE-LIS DESIGNS ON ROBE

TRADITIONAL VESTMENT COLORS: RED ROBE, BLUE MANTLE

INFRARED SHOWS APPARENT UNDERDRAWING

The Image of Guadalupe

Figure 14. Supposedly a "miraculous" portrait of the Virgin Mary, the Image of Guadalupe actually exhibits artistic motifs and evidence of painting, even in its "original" areas.

time the Guadalupan Image appeared, some Renaissance artists had begun to work without preliminary sketching.[49]

In any case, there may indeed be evidence of underdrawing. Callahan concedes that infrared photographs of the robe's fold shadows reveal what "may, under cursory examination, appear to be thin sketch lines." But he argues that because they are actually "broad and also blended with the paint," they are "uncharacteristic of undersketching."[50] He fails to explain—as we think the onus is on him to do—what the anomalous lines *are* characteristic of. We feel that they do appear to be sketch lines, their breadth merely suggesting that the drawing was performed with a brush or was "fixed" with a brush; any "blending" could well be the result of the undersketching having been done in a soluble medium that was partially dissolved and disturbed by subsequent overpainting.

Even if we accept Smith's and Callahan's assertions that there is no underdrawing and that a number of obvious artistic motifs are later additions, there still remains strong evidence that the Image is a painting. For one thing, the "original," supposedly miraculous areas still contain obvious artistic motifs and conventions: the formulaic, *contrapposto* stance of the figure; the Virgin's familiarly tilted head and downcast gaze (as in Raphael's *Madonna del Granduca* and countless other paintings); and the traditional vestment colors of the Madonna, the robe or tunic of red and the mantle of blue. Earlier we mentioned that the flesh tones are in the "Dark Virgin" tradition.[51]

Especially noteworthy is the position of the hands, pressed together in the familiar attitude of prayer. Smith and Callahan seem unaware that this gesture would have been foreign to the mother of Jesus, who would be expected to pray in the ancient manner. As this is represented in the earliest Christian art, the two arms are raised symmetrically in a gesture of supplication.[52] According to M. D. Anderson, "The posture with hands joined was unknown alike to pagan antiquity and early Christianity; it appears in the eighth century but did not become common until the twelfth century."[53]

In short, the motif seems merely a convention that an artist of the sixteenth century would naturally have adopted and, with the other motifs and conventions, lessens the credibility of the "miraculous" appearance.

Evidence that the Image is a mere painting dates from as early as 1556. In testimony given during the formal investigation of the cloth in that year, Father Alonzo de Santiago stated that the Image was "painted yesteryear by an Indian." Another Franciscan priest, Juan de Maseques, supplied more specific information, testifying that the Image "was a painting that the Indian painter Marcos had done." Smith does admit that there was an Aztec painter known as Marcos Cipac active in Mexico at the time the Image appeared. Whether or not he was still living in 1556 when he was accused of painting the Image is uncertain. What is known is that Marcos did not attend the inquiry to deny the accusation.[54]

More recent evidence of painting comes from an examination of Callahan's visible-light and infrared photographs.[55] We were assisted in this by Glenn Taylor, a professional artist with many years' experience in an impressive variety of portraiture techniques. We asked him to concentrate on the "original" portions of the Image, and he made a number of observations: that the part in the Virgin of Guadalupe's hair is off-center and suggestive of amateur artwork; that her eyes, including the irises, have outlines, as they often do in paintings but not in nature, and that these outlines appear to have been done with a brush; and that the Virgin's traditional likeness, *contrapposto* stance, and other elements were indicative of European paintings of the Renaissance era. To him, "The detailing of the features exhibits the characteristic fluidity of painting." He describes the work as obviously "mannered" (in the artistic sense) and suggests it was probably copied by an inexpert copyist from an expertly done original.[56]

One of the silliest examples of "scientific research" being conducted on the Guadalupan Image—by "several ophthalmologists" and "a computer expert"—takes the *acheiropoietos* tradition from the macroscopic to the microscopic level. It concerns "what seems to be the reflected image of a man's head in the right eye of the Virgin" (as Smith describes it), what was once thought to be Juan Diego's own portrait in magical miniature, until someone realized that Aztecs of the time were clean-shaven; thereupon it was re-interpreted as "a bearded Spaniard." Now, with the aid of photo-enhancement techniques (akin to those applied to the Turin "shroud" in hopes of identifying wished-for "Roman coins" over the eyes), still more tiny figures are being "discovered" and assigned to various sixteenth-century Mexican personages, such as Bishop Zumarraga. Meanwhile, the specific methodology is being questioned.[57] And at one point in his own discussion of the endeavor, Smith does wonder whether the proliferating wee people represent anything more "substantial than the human shapes we see in the clouds, the result of what Father Harold J. Rahn once termed a 'pious imagination'.["58] The whole protracted affair is reminiscent of those who saw the "face of Christ" on a New Mexico tortilla in 1978,[59] and again in the wood grain of an Alabama hospital door in 1983.[60]

SUMMARY, CONCLUSIONS, AND RECOMMENDATIONS

In summary, we believe that our two-pronged investigation has presented overwhelming evidence against the claims of authenticity, casting doubt on the genuineness of both legend and image. In the former, we observe the familiar biblical motifs; realize that the larger story—complete with the name Guadalupe—was almost surely borrowed from a similar Spanish one; understand that the concept is in the infamous tradition of "not-made-with-hands" portraits and other "miraculous" depictions of Mary; and recognize the elements of religious dogma such as hyperdulia and "perpetual virginity." All of these, especially when taken together, suggest deliberate manufacture.

So does the image itself, which has—even in the supposedly "original" and "miraculous" areas—stock artistic motifs and apparent underdrawing; copious amounts of what appear to be pigments; and cracking and flaking such as occurs with paint. The strong European elements—together with the evidence of amateurishness in rendering them—support Glenn Taylor's suggestion that the Image was largely copied from a more expert work or works. That the artist was an Indian is suggested by a supposed Aztec motif (the particular lower fold of the Virgin's robe), the apparent Aztec source of the blue pigment, and possibly even the complexion of the Virgin. (Although that can be equally explained by the "Dark Virgin" tradition, it would seem that that particular tradition might have been chosen because of its expected appeal to the Indian population.) Besides, we even have the testimony of two contemporary priests that the Image was done by a native artist, and of one of them that it was painted by "the Indian painter Marcos."

In conclusion, the Church's desire to convert the Aztecs would seem to have been the motive, and the fact that the Indians had a similar Virgin goddess provided the opportunity. The means was the "miracle" (baldly taken from the Spanish Guadalupan legend) and—to complete our case—the Image is the smoking gun. We say this because nowhere is there convincing evidence of its supposedly miraculous nature, but everywhere signs of human artistry and fraud.

Nevertheless, should Guadalupan researchers desire to apply true science to the question of authenticity, we have some positive suggestions. We recommend that direct sampling of the Image—especially of the supposedly "miraculous" portions—should be undertaken. This can be accomplished by careful sampling of minute amounts of coloring matter, so minute as to be indetectible to the unaided eye. Then, in addition to such standard techniques as polarized-light microscopy, scanning electron microprobe analysis, and various microchemical tests, we would suggest the application of Fourier transform infrared technology (FTIR), which is proving a valuable research technique.[61] We are aware that spectrophotometry has reportedly been done,[62] but the results are apparently still not available. We believe that attempts to identify any pigments (or mixtures of pigments) and any binding media, etc., *in situ*— that is, without actual removal of samples—would be so potentially error-prone as to further exacerbate the controversy rather than resolve it. Furthermore, we strongly recommend that further testing be conducted by impartial, independent laboratories rather than by the present examiners.

Select Bibliography

Burrus, Ernest T. *The Oldest Copy of the Nican Mopohua.* Washington, D.C.: Center for Applied Research in the Apostolate, 1981. A discussion of the oldest manuscript account (ca. 1551-1561) of the Virgin's appearance to Juan Diego.

Callahan, Philip Serna. *The Tilma under Infra-red Radiation.* Washington, D.C.: Center for Applied Research in the Apostolate, 1981. A collection of infra-red photographs and a discussion of how they supposedly support the claim that the Image of Guadalupe was not painted.

LaFaye, Jacques. *Quetzalcoatl and Guadalupe: The Formation of Mexican National Consciousness 1531-1813,* 231–253. Chicago: University of Chicago Press, 1976. A historical work that points out the similarity between the Mexican story of the origin of the Guadalupan Image and an earlier Spanish legend, which probably prompted the tale.

Smith, Jody Brant. *The Image of Guadalupe.* Garden City, N.Y.: Doubleday, 1983. A popular book-length treatment, exaggerating aspects of the claim for a miraculous origin of the image; does provide necessary historical details, including early testimony the image was the work of a native artist.

Tierney, Patrick. "The Arts." *Omni,* September 1983, 174, 190. A brief account critical of the methodology used to "discover" tiny images of sixteenth-century Mexican personages in the eyes of the Guadalupan Image.

Acknowledgments

This chapter originally appeared as "The Image of Guadalupe: A Folkloristic and Iconographic Investigation," in the *Skeptical Inquirer,* Vol. 8, No. 4 (Spring 1985), pp. 243-255.

The authors wish to thank Michael Schneider of Research Devices, Inc. (Berkeley Heights, N.J.) for his technical assistance; D. Scott Rogo (Northridge, Calif.) for providing essential source material; Lina Crocker (University of Kentucky) for help in translating from the Spanish; and Glenn Taylor (Lexington, Ky.) for his professional opinions.

9. BLEEDING DOOR
Enigma on Deadening Branch

The question now is about haemoglobin.

—SHERLOCK HOLMES
A Study in Scarlet

Can objects and images associated with bloody deaths actually *bleed?* Yes, say those who would pit the supernatural against science, recounting instances of stones and paintings that yield flows of apparent blood, and (ironically) citing scientific tests that confirm the identity.

Tales of such supposedly supernatural occurrences are widespread. In classical mythology, when Triopas's son, Erysichthon, cut down a sacred oak—in which lived a Dryad—blood flowed from the ax's cuts.[1] Again, on an occasion when Aeneas and his men gathered myrtle, they saw that the wood was bleeding and heard the voice of Polydorus call out from his unmarked grave.[2]

Not surprising, perhaps, religions which venerate images of bloody martyrdom often yield claims of miraculous occurrences involving blood. For example, for several years beginning in 1911, at the home of a French abbé, blood flowed from both a picture and a statue of Christ, and also dripped from hosts (wafers) that the abbé had consecrated. Under observation by an investigator, however, the picture failed to bleed,

---

Investigated with John F. Fischer.

and when it did become wet with blood after being locked in the chapel, the investigator found that a piece of paper that he had secretly placed in the door hinge had been dislodged. On one occasion, analysis showed that the substance was not genuine blood, and on another, the investigator's wife thought she saw the abbé secretly sprinkle water on the picture from a vase just prior to her husband's examination. (Possibly, dried blood was already placed on the picture and the water was all that was necessary to give the illusion of fresh blood. Despite such evidence, however, the investigator could never bring himself to believe that the pious old man was capable of deceit.)[3]

Among many similar cases was one that transpired in 1985 when a two-foot-high statue of the Virgin Mary owned by a railroad worker in Quebec began to weep first tears and then blood. The phenomena began on December 8, the feast of the Immaculate Conception, and soon spread to nearby statues, icons, and crucifixes. In less than a week the "miracle" drew an estimated 12,000 people, who lined up for hours in sub-zero temperatures.[4] The hoax was later exposed (a mixture of beef fat and blood would flow when the room became heated).

If pious testimony is to be believed, a block of marble enshrined in a church in Pozzuoli, Italy—and reputed to be the very stone upon which St. Januarius was beheaded—has sometimes exuded human blood. Although rare, when the phenomenon does occur it reportedly coincides with celebrations held in the martyr's honor in Naples. (Occasionally during these celebrations the saint's coagulated "blood" is seen to liquefy in one of the two vials containing it, a phenomenon treated with considerable skepticism by such sources as Brewer's *Dictionary of Miracles*.)[5]

Whether the alleged phenomenon is miracle or religious hoax, the story of the Pozzuoli stone contains *motifs* (or narrative elements) common to legends and well known to folklorists: "Revenant [i.e., ghost] as blood" and "Ineradicable bloodstain after bloody tragedy."[6]

There are many such tales in which, typically, the "ineradicable" quality of the stain is dramatized. For example, there is the story of Castle Lockenhaus in Austria, whose sixteenth-century owner, a Countess Bathori, was rumored to have murdered young girls and to have drunk their blood. Under the castle arch is a faint, brownish patch of earth that turns blood-red whenever rain falls on it. "Efforts have been made to remove the stain, but without avail. Some mysterious power has given it a permanence that defies explanation and the power of modern science to get rid of it."[7] Or so the castle's caretaker tells credulous tourists.

Another indellible-stain story concerns a convicted Pennsylvania murderer, Thomas P. Fisher, who went to his execution in 1878 protesting his innocence. According to one source:

> As he was being dragged away to be hanged he managed to cut his hand and, allowing the blood to flow freely, planted it firmly on the wall of his cell, shouting, "My mark will stay here as long as this prison remains." Repeated painting and whitewashing have failed to remove the outline of a man's hand, marked in blood.[8]

My own encounter with such phenomena occurred in 1978. It involved an eastern Kentucky farmhouse with mysterious sounds and a door that "bleeds"—all attributed to a century-old tragedy—plus a location with the curious name "Deadening Branch."[9]

In the last century a family by the name of Eversole reportedly occupied the farm and, in season, operated a small sugar cane mill near the house. The family included a young boy, about nine or ten years old.

One day, goes the story, tragedy struck: The lad went alone to the mill, hitched the mule to the "sweep," and began to feed stalks of cane into the press. Somehow—no one knows the exact details—the boy was caught and crushed to death. Supposedly the youth's body was "laid out" on a door and later buried on a hill overlooking the farm.

My late father and I heard the story one rainy day in a country store while we were out gathering data on local cemeteries and recording tombstone inscriptions for a historical society project. An eldery resident who lived near the farm also told of the "hant" that was said to roam the now-deserted farm. The "hant," he said, was responsible for some mighty strange goings-on.

According to him, there had been a variety of inexplicable occurrences. After a rain, the cane mill—long vanished—could still be heard, operating with a characteristic creaking sound! Also after a rain, we were told, mysterious blood-like streaks could be seen oozing through the paint on the front door!

Other mysteries centered around that door. One day while working with some men just across the creek from the house, our informant heard the door banging back and forth. The workmen looked as the sounds continued briefly, but they were certain the door hadn't moved. And the wind was quite still.

Another in the small group at the country store, a young man, was reminded of his own curious experience with the ghost. He was hunting in the vicinity and he too heard a banging sound. He described it as "like someone stacking lumber" (or, as another suggested helpfully, perhaps "like someone building a coffin"). He checked, and found no one there.

I was intrigued by the stories, and expressed an interest in the house with the bleeding door, observing aloud that the day was a fine one for a visit, since it had just stopped raining. The young man offered at once to show us the farm, but cautioned that much of the "road" to it was no more than a rocky creek bed. This presented no problem, since my father had his four-wheel-drive vehicle and he too liked a good story and an excuse for an outing. Besides, we would have the opportunity to check out another cemetery for our project.

So off we went. The young man confessed that he did not relish visiting the house alone, although he did not mind with us along. We soon encountered a "NO TRESPASSING" sign, but our guide assured us that the owner would not object to our visit. We parked near the barn, which we were told had been built on the site of the old cane mill.

As we approached the house (see Figure 15), I listened carefully for any strange noises, but there were none. With only a glance at the house—there *were* dark streaks on the door (see Figure 16)!—the young man led on through the tall, wet weeds and through the woods to the top of the hill, where we found the long-abandoned burial ground. I had my notepad for recording any tombstone data and some chalk for enhancing weathered inscriptions, but these were unnecessary: The several graves, badly sunken, were marked only with common fieldstones. We examined each one carefully, scraping off lichens and moss where necessary, in hopes of finding some crude lettering—perhaps an initial "E" for the family name of Eversole. But there was nothing.

We returned to the house for a closer inspection. My father cautioned me to be careful as I climbed the fragile stairs to the attic and listened: Again nothing.

The house had obviously been used in past years for storing tobacco for curing. Long two-by-four planks had been nailed up to serve as

Figure 15. Deserted farmhouse on Deadening Branch in eastern Kentucky, reportedly site of various mysterious phenomena. (Photograph by author)

Figure 16. "Bleeding" door does exhibit dark streaks that recall century-old tragedy, the door allegedly having been used to support a child's mangled corpse.

racks for hanging the tobacco. And a front room even had the side window enlarged into an open doorway for easy access.

It was while our companion and I were standing in this room that the "hant" became manifest: Bam! Bam-bam-bam-bam-bam! We looked at each other, and our guide gave a sheepish look. The door to the room had been opened against one of the two-by-fours, and a momentary gentle breeze had drifted up the branch, through the side opening, rattling the door against the plank. The gust spent, the noise ceased.

The reverberating of the long board would, from a distance away, sound just like the clatter of "someone stacking lumber." Indeed, without any prompting from me, the young man stated that surely that very sound was what he had heard on the earlier occasion. We knew, too, that it would also account for the sounds the group of workmen had heard. In this instance, as then, the *front* door had not moved at all.

Next we investigated the mysterious "blood." We saw that the grayish stain started at the top and separated into two streaks continuing about halfway down the door. Most suggestive, the streaks were below corresponding points on the overhead casing where water collected briefly after running off the roof before washing onto the door. Clearly, we were not dealing with blood, but rather with water-borne substances— possibly tar, decaying leaves, dirt, etc.—washing down from the roof. But—ever wishing to be thorough—I very lightly scraped off some of this deposit, wrapping it carefully in paper and placing it in my pocket for future analysis.

We did not witness the alleged "creaking" of the "cane mill," but there was a ready explanation for that sound in any case. Since the barn was built on the site of the original structure, and since it was in dilapidated condition with rusting hinges and warped boards hanging from old nails, there were opportunities aplenty for creaking noises. Naturally, however, one could not expect them always to perform on cue as the inner door so conveniently had.

In the days after our first visit, I did some further research. At the local library I searched through old census records on microfilm until my eyes were bleary. I had hopes of finding confirmation that an Eversole family had once lived in the area. For 1830, 1840, 1850, 1860 and 1870, there was none,[10] but at length I found what I was looking for. In the 1880 census was a John Eversole, age twenty-five, a farmer. Listed in the family were his wife, Rachel (three years his senior), and their three children, Mary J. (age six), Eliza A. (four), and Marcus N. (one).[11]

Could one-year-old Marcus Eversole have been—a decade later— the victim of the tragedy? Was it little Marcus who had supposedly become a "hant?" Imagine my frustration at the fact that the 1890 census records (along with those of most of the United States for that census) had been destroyed by fire in Washington. The 1900 census listed no Eversole family in the county, and it is possible that they moved elsewhere after the reported tragedy. At least I had confirmation that there had been an Eversole family with a young boy, and thus an approximate date for the child's death as circa 1889. Our elderly informant had originally placed the event somewhat earlier, but he readily accepted the revised date as more likely to be correct and seemed pleased at the documentation.

My father pinpointed the farm for me on one of his topographic maps, which graphically illustrated a feature of the area: Several small side hollows converged in the immediate vicinity of the old farmhouse. I guessed that noises in the area might be amplified or multiplied by an echo effect (as there had been at Mackenzie House) when listeners were standing in certain other locations. A second visit to the farm enabled me to experience some proof of that possibility and to take photographs.

But had little more than a few noises inspired a full-blown tale of haunting? Not entirely, perhaps. The story contains many common folk motifs, as I soon learned by comparing it with other traditional ghost stories.[12] Among the motifs are the following (with their standard folk-motif numbers[13]):

- Ghost haunts place of great accident or misfortune (E275)
- Ghost haunts house (E281)
- Sounds of accident reenact tragedy (E337.1.2)
- Invisible ghost makes rapping or knocking noise (E402.1.5)
- Persons who die violent or accidental deaths cannot rest in grave (E411.10)

And there are others.

The stock motifs suggest the possibility that the story was strongly influenced by a general climate in which ghost stories are told with relish, and in which narrative elements may even migrate from tale to tale.

The same may be said of the central motifs, "Revenant as blood" (E422.1.11.5) and "Ineradicable bloodstain after bloody tragedy" (E 22.1.11.5.1). (I have heard at least three other indellible-bloodstain stories in central and eastern Kentucky, and I suspect they are common.)

Of course blood can soak into unpainted wood to a depth that can indeed render the stain relatively "ineradicable," but stories like the foregoing are imbued with supernatural overtones that reflect cultural attitudes toward blood. According to *Funk & Wagnall's Standard Dictionary of Folklore, Mythology and Legend*:

Primitive men generally look on blood as being life itself. They see blood flow and the body die and therefore assume that life flows out of the body in a literal sense. Closely allied to this is the belief that the soul or spirit of the being is in his blood, and that when blood escapes the blood-soul escapes too.[14]

As a consequence, a proliferation of superstitions and taboos, as well as rituals and magical practices, have arisen in association with blood.[15]

In light of all this, one wonders: Did the detail in the Eversole story—that the boy's body was placed on a door—occur before or after the "blood" stains were observed? One reason to suspect that it was *after* is to note that it is a rather precise (as well as unlikely) detail in a story with many otherwise stock elements. Perhaps once the stain was noted, someone suggested an explanation (first offered as supposition, then, in the later retellings, adopted as fact): A door *could* be used for carrying a crushed and mangled corpse.

Another point: Was the "creaking" of the cane mill (as a motif, the reenactment of the tragedy) actually heard, or only imagined due to the power of suggestion? Could it not have been expected to have entered the story in any case?

After the field work and the research with old records and maps and books, it remained for forensic science to play its part. I therefore submitted the scrapings from the door stains for microchemical analysis. (This was, in fact, the very first case I worked on with John Fischer, who had been highly recommended to me by a commercial laboratory. We thus began a friendship and partnership that has involved us for a decade in many challenging investigations.)

Now every day in forensic laboratories around the world, countless "blood" specimens are received for testing. Often they have been submitted with no more justification than that the stains are of a reddish-brown color resembling blood, or that—as in this case, where they were blackish like old blood—the stains are simply unidentified, yet had been in a context that raised the question of blood.

Whenever such an issue is at hand, before any tests are conducted to determine whether the stain may be human blood or, if so, what type it may be, the procedure is first to attempt to identify the substance *as* blood. Only if the results are positive are further tests then warranted.

The preliminary tests, which are for various hemoglobin-related compounds, consist of the application of certain reagents that yield color or other reactions in the presence of the compounds. Often, when the amount of blood may be tiny, the tests are conducted under microscopic observation.

With the samples I had submitted, several such tests indicated that no blood was present, even in trace amounts. And so another tale of the supernatural succumbed to investigation and gave up the ghost.

Select Bibliography

Brewer, E. Cobham. *Dictionary of Miracles,* 184. Philadelphia: Lippincott, 1884. A nineteenth-century reference work on alleged miracles including a skeptical view of the liquefying blood of St. Januarius in Naples.

Rogo, D. Scott. *Miracles.* New York: Dial Press, 1982. A parapsychologist's look at such religious enigmas as bleeding icons, stigmata, "divine" images, "miraculous" healings, etc.

Thompson, Stith. *Motif-Index of Folk Literature.* Rev. ed. 6 vols. Bloomington: Indiana University Press, 1955. A standard reference work cataloging folk motifs (the smallest units of narrative folklore), e.g., "revenant as blood," "ineradicable bloodstain after bloody tragedy," etc.

Acknowledgments

Thanks are due Boyd Keeton and Dallas Sparks, Crockett, Kentucky, for their help with this case. We are also grateful once again to Robert H. van Outer for his photographic assistance.

10. RESTLESS COFFINS
The Barbados Vault Mystery

What is this haunted crypt?

—SHERLOCK HOLMES
"The Adventure of Shoscombe Old Place"

It has been labeled "one of the great riddles of the last century."[1] Indeed, few mysteries of the "strange" variety have generated such interest or have gone unsolved for so long as the celebrated mystery of the "restless coffins" of Barbados. The story has been told countless times, at greatest length by Rupert T. Gould in his popular *Oddities* (1928).[2]

Briefly, on several occasions between 1812 and 1820 the Chase Vault (see Figure 17) was opened to receive a new coffin. Typically, the other coffins would be found in a "confused state," as if they had been "tossed" from their places! No satisfactory explanation was ever found.

The earliest-known published account is by Sir J. E. Alexander in his *Transatlantic Sketches* (1833). As he says:

Each time that the vault was opened the coffins were replaced in their proper situations, that is, three on the ground side by side, and the others laid on them. The vault was then regularly closed; the door (a massive stone which required six or seven men to move) was cemented by masons; and though the floor was of sand, there were no marks or foot-steps or water.

The Chase Vault
circa 1812-20

Figure 17. Burial vault on the island of Barbados. Each time the sealed crypt was opened, the coffins were found in strange disarray.

Alexander adds:

> The last time the vault was opened was in 1819. Lord Combermere [Governor of the colony] was then present, and the coffins were found confusedly thrown about the vault, some with their heads down and others up. What could have occasioned this phenomenon? In no other vault in the island has this ever occurred. Was it an earthquake which occasioned it, or the effects of an inundation in the vault?[3]

Today, on the island of Barbados, from its location in the churchyard of Christ Church, on an eminence overlooking Oistin's Bay, the Chase Vault stands open and empty, providing no hint of the mysterious phenomena attributed to it more than a century and a half ago.

But the years have not been silent; and, as the tale has been told repeatedly, it has often been "improved" in the retelling. As Sir Algernon Aspinall wrote in 1915, in his *West Indian Tales of Old*:

> Though the salient features of the several versions of the "Barbados Coffin Story" are the same, the details vary greatly. To such an extent, indeed, has the story been twisted and turned about to suit the styles of individual writers and the tastes of their readers, that it is difficult to winnow the true grain of fact from the chaff of descriptive colouring.[4]

Actually, it is a challenge to find two versions of the tale which quite agree. For example, Alexander records that the last opening of the vault was in 1819, while other accounts give 1820. There are further discrepancies between the various accounts as to dates, number of persons interred, position of the coffins, number of disturbances, and so on.

Aspinall reports that "a recently unearthed manuscript of the late Hon. Nathan Lucas . . . now furnishes the only really dependable account."[5] Unfortunately, although Lucas vows that he was an eyewitness to the last opening, he is forced to rely on Rev. Thomas H. Orderson's account of the earlier incidents; and Orderson himself (if several "authentic" accounts allegedly signed by him can be believed) never told the story quite the same way twice. For example, one of Orderson's versions, says Gould, "omits an important interment in the vault altogether, and gives a wrong date for the first appearance of the disturbances."[6]

I will not burden the reader with all the details and variants of the details in the several "authentic" versions except to note that the Lucas/Orderson account records seven interments (from 1807 to 1819) and (beginning with the opening of the vault on the occasion of the third burial, in 1812) four disturbances. The coffins were leaden ones except for two wooden coffins—one of which (that of a Mrs. Goddard) "had fallen to pieces and was tied up in a small bundle,"[7] the other wooden coffin having been the last interred. Reportedly, only the *leaden* coffins were disturbed, the wooden ones remaining in place.

In 1819 Lord Combermere had supposedly sanded the floor of the vault to detect footprints of any intruders. This detail—widely cited in modern accounts—is doubtful. It is not mentioned in the Lucas/Orderson version, termed "the earliest known record of the Barbados Mystery."[8] And the first *published* account (Alexander's) states not that sand was put down but that "the floor was of sand,"[9] which in any case is untrue. It may have been Sir Robert Schomburgk who (in his 1848 *History of Barbados*) first "improved" upon this detail, supplying what was omitted by both Lucas and Orderson (possibly because it had never transpired) and "correcting" Alexander's obvious error. Schomburgk claims that "fine sand [later writers have somehow "discovered" that it was "white sand" and even "soft white beach sand"] was thrown over the floor of the vault, so that, if a person should enter it from any other part than the usual entrance, marks might be left behind."[10]

In any event, Lord Combermere had reportedly had the stone slab covering the entrance sealed, and several of those present had placed their "private marks" in the fresh cement.[11] (Much later accounts— including one supposedly verified by Combermere—would add that the "governor's seal" was employed.[12]) There was no evidence of entry or of tampering with the vault when it was last opened, in 1820.

Even the "really dependable account" by Lucas/Orderson cannot be taken entirely at face value. There is, for instance, at least one minor internal inconsistency. Rev. Orderson states that "on April 20th, 1820 the bundle [of Mrs. Goddard's coffin] was *in situ*"; however, a few paragraphs later he states, "Since the 18th [sic] of April 1920 all the coffins have been removed from the vault . . . and have been buried in a grave. . . ."[13]

There are other problems, one of which concerns a drawing accompanying the Lucas/Orderson account, which shows the position of the scrambled coffins on the last opening of the vault. This, says Lucas, was "made for me at the instance of the Doctor [the Rev. Dr. Orderson], copied from one sketched on the spot by the Honble Major Finck who very soon joined our party at the vault."[14] But as Gould observes: "The [Lucas statement] does not say in what state any of the coffins were found; it merely refers to 'the annexed drawing.' In this, the Clarke coffin is shown undisturbed, and that of Samuel Brewster also. This fact casts some doubt on the authenticity of the drawing." Gould adds: "Such a striking exception as two coffins left untouched out of six would surely, one thinks, have been commented on in the other narratives."[15]

Furthermore, the "bundle" of Mrs. Goddard's coffin is not depicted at all. (Neither is it shown in any of the sketches accompanying the different accounts. And, incidentally, none of the sketches can be reconciled with each other as to the position of the disturbed coffins at the final opening. One, for instance, said to be made by an eyewitness, does not bear any similarity to the Finck/Orderson drawing.[16])

Moreover, in the Lucas manuscript, Rev. Orderson states that in 1812 an infant's coffin "was nearly upright in the corner, but the head was down to the ground," whereas the "annexed drawing" clearly shows the foot of the coffin resting on the floor.[17]

Yet another discrepancy was noted by Gould:

> . . . It seems generally agreed that the three largest coffins were laid side by side on the floor of the vault, and the other three arranged one on top of each of these. The only divergent account is that given by Lucas, who states: "The children's coffins were placed upon bricks in the Vault; Mr. Chase's on the Rock, the bottom of the Vault." This is entirely at variance with the sketches accompanying his account.[18]

So if the Lucas/Orderson version is really the most "dependable," we are indeed on uncertain ground. Still, most authors have argued (primarily on the supposition that all those reputable people wouldn't lie) that "the evidence for the bulk of the happenings"—as Gould confidently asserts—"is quite unassailable."[19]

With that in mind, I began an investigation of the unsolved mystery—an investigation that would span more than two years. Unable to travel to Barbados myself, I relied on the examinations of the vault made by others. I commissioned a Barbadian researcher, Mrs. G. R. Hamilton, to conduct several inquiries for me. In addition I was aided in my research by Barbadian and American experts and archivists. And Mr. Hugh Foster of the Barbados Department of Tourism was most helpful in expediting several inquiries.

While beginning to check on the veracity of the early accounts, I also sought to form a working hypothesis to explain the mysterious phenomena. It was apparent that either (A) the story was not true as reported, or (B) the story was essentially true. If the latter were correct, then the events had (a) a natural explanation (including the possibility of human agency), or (b) a paranormal explanation.

The postulation of a paranormal or supernatural explanation would only be justified after all natural (or human) causes had been decisively eliminated. In any case, if some paranormal agency were responsible, it was difficult to categorize it—spiritualistic manifestations? poltergeist phenomena? West Indian voodoo?—and even proponents of such phenomena were somewhat reserved in suggesting them in this instance.

True, there were other, similar "restless coffins" stories reported elsewhere (on which more later); but again, no common explanation—paranormal or otherwise—could be agreed upon. I therefore opted to focus on the Barbados case with naturalistic hypotheses in mind—a necessarily short list of which was offered by Gould.[20] Here follows a brief summary:

Human agency. Once discounted by almost all researchers, this was again suggested in recent years by Iris Owen of the Toronto Society for Psychical Research, who concluded (in the April 1975 *New Horizons*): "My own personal feeling is that the vault was entered from the back [by slaves] from motives of revenge at ill treatment. The matter of the undisturbed sand floor is easily explained—nothing would be simpler than to spread fresh sand behind on leaving!"[21] But long ago Gould argued that the local slaves were too superstitious to break into a tomb, and that in any case, if revenge were the motive, "it is difficult to imagine why they (there must have been more than one) should have contented themselves with merely throwing the coffins about, and not have attempted to open them for the purpose of mutilating or defiling their occupants."[22] As to any presumed motive of grave robbery, that notion, says John Godwin (*This Baffling World*, 1968), "can be discarded. All the people concerned were Anglicans, and were buried without valuables." And, echoing Gould, he adds," If it was a human agency that shifted the coffins, those hands could just as well have forced them open. Yet all the lids remained in place."[23]

Earthquakes. This has, correctly I think, been quickly discounted. A series of earthquakes, so localized as to affect only one vault—and always the same one—is patently ridiculous, as is, incidentally, the suggestion of lightning as the cause.

Escaping gasses. Gasses from decomposing bodies represented a possibility suggested by Gould "only for the sake of completeness." As he observed, ". . . no volume of gas that could conceivably be generated would be able, even if it escaped suddenly at a single small vent, to produce any motion of the coffin in which it had been confined; unless, indeed, the latter were . . . [somehow] relieved of the effects of weight and friction."[24] To suggest that several coffins would be repeatedly so moved—and to the extent (if the detail is to be believed) of standing one coffin on end—is ludicrous.

Flooding. Gould cites evidence that even leaden coffins will float, and mentions the Gretford, England, case of shifting coffins (of lead cased in wood, whereas in Barbados they were of wood cased in lead) in which flooding was suspected.

Gould suggests that a brief inundation of the vault might not leave obvious traces if it were of short duration. The flooding theory, he says,

> . . . provides a natural explanation of the whole mystery; it produces an agency of quite sufficient power to displace the coffins, overturn them, and even stand them head downwards; and it does not involve any disarrangement either of seals or private marks on the outside of the vault or of the material strewn on the floor for the purpose of detecting foot-marks.

But, he notes, flooding was specifically considered by Lord Combermere's party. According to Lucas: "There was no vestige of water to be discovered in the vault; no mark where it had been; and the vault is in a level Church Yard, by no means in a fall much less than a run of water."

Gould further states that "all but two feet of the vault was above the ground-level," and that a maximum of only two feet of water would be insufficient to float stacked coffins.[25]

But here Gould and those after him are in error. They are relying on Orderson's statement, "The vault is dug in the ground about two feet in the lime rock."[26] Photos of the vault indicated otherwise to me. The width and length of the vault (6½ feet by 12 feet) served as a scale by which I determined that much of the vault was obviously below ground. And in answer to my query, Hugh Foster wrote me confirming that "the distance between the floor of the vault and the level of the ground outside is eight (8) feet."[27]

Apparently Orderson simply meant that the vault—in addition to being "dug in the ground"—had been continued downward into the rock an *additional* two feet. And so, given a source for the water, the flooding hypothesis deserved to be taken seriously once again.

I therefore posed the problem to the Chief Engineer of the Waterworks Department, Government of Barbados, and received this information:

Ground water in Barbados occurs as a thick lens averaging about 40 to 60 feet in thickness, and extending along the west and south coasts of the island. The fresh water, because of its lower specific gravity, floats on the heavier salt water, and extends inland to an average distance of three miles.

The significant characteristic of the island's ground water where your inquiry is concerned, is that the top of the water table is at sea level. Consequently, the higher the ground elevation, the greater would be the depth to the ground water aquifer. For example, if the Chase Vault were at a ground elevation of say 200 feet, then the ground water would be 200 feet below the vault, flooding would therefore be an absolute impossibility. For flooding to be a real possibility, the vault would have to be no more than a few feet above sea level. In this latter case, the seasonal fluctuations in the ground water levels which occur (generally up to four feet) could result in flooding.

He added that "to summarize the argument above, the possibility of flooding hinges on the location of the vault with respect to sea level. If the vault were located more than ten feet above sea level, then flooding could not have been the cause of the movements" of the coffins in the Chase Vault.

Thus, since the churchyard is high above sea level (Iris Owen states it is "some 250 feet"), the possibility of inundation by groundwater must be ruled out. The engineer replied to a further query by stating that, No, he could "not conceive of any conditions under which water might have inundated the vault in sufficient degree" to have floated the coffins.[28]

If the cause of the disturbances was not flooding of the vault, then what could it have been? Or was the story fraudulent after all?

As reported by Aspinall, a Mr. Forster Alleyne had done extensive research on the matter. Although it has been reported that news of the strange disturbances had spread to "all of the British West Indies" and that "throngs of sightseers flocked to the graveyard" and "crowded around the vault," the fact is that Alleyne searched the files of contemporary newspapers without finding any mention of the sensational mystery. There was likewise nothing in the Parochial Treasurer's accounts, nor in the Register of Burials of Christ Church. As to the latter, Alleyne did find the entries for those interred during the period concerned, but with "absolutely no comment" nor "the smallest hint that anything extraordinary had taken place."[29]

Nor did any master copy of Orderson's account turn up—such having been suggested by Gould as a means to rationalize the divergent accounts. As Gould theorized, "Mr. Orderson seems first to have drawn up a complete account for his own reference and then, at different times, to have made several copies of this for curious correspondents. As time went on, he may have grown weary of the whole subject . . ." and thereby have become careless in dashing off the "authentic" accounts.[30]

Be that as it may, Aspinall himself observed, "It is curious that Isaac W. Orderson, the Rector's brother, should have made no mention of the mystery"[31] in his volume, *Creoleana, or Social and Domestic Scenes and Incidents in Barbados in Days of Yore*, published in London in 1842.

I shared Aspinall's curiosity, and so obtained, with some difficulty, a copy of Isaac Orderson's book. Aspinall was right: Although the volume covered the period in question, there was not the slightest hint of the Barbados coffins mystery. I wondered why.

Perhaps it was because Isaac Orderson had, as he said in his preface, determined to tell only those stories of Barbados which were true! In his own words: "With regard to the contents of the present volume, the Author conscientiously affirms, that his materials are all (with the exception of one incident) drawn from facts, which are as closely adhered to as the nature of the subject would admit. . . ."[32]

It seems to me unthinkable that Isaac Orderson could not have *known* of such a series of fantastic occurrences as the disturbances in the Chase Vault, especially since the story had been published and since his brother had, allegedly, figured so prominently in the incidents. And since he must surely have known of the fascinating tale, it seems unlikely in the extreme that he should omit to mention it, unless he knew (and knew firsthand) what we can only suppose on the evidence—that the coffins story was untrue.

Alleyne and Aspinall failed to heed the warning inherent in Isaac Orderson's omission, possibly because they strongly wished the tale to be true and also because Alleyne had unearthed the Lucas manuscript. Yet we have already seen how very doubtful that account is.

It was at this point in my investigation—thoroughly sobered by the preponderance of negative evidence—that I noted a suggestive little detail, one that was soon to set me on a path toward a solution to the famous mystery. Whereas some modern authors refer to "workmen" who examined the vault and unsealed and resealed the stone slab with cement, the earlier accounts invariably refer to them as "masons." And "masons" are much more active in the earlier narratives than in the recent ones. To understand the significance of this seemingly minor point, it will be necessary to make a brief digression.

I had earlier investigated a legend of buried treasure, that of the "lost silver mines" of one "Jonathan Swift," in the folklore of Kentucky and neighboring states. In his purported *Journal*, "Swift" (whose existence cannot be proved historically) states that he marked a tree with "the symbols of a compass [some versions read "compasses"], trowel and square." Now the combined *compass* (a drawing compass, or "pair of compasses") and *square* represent the emblem of the secret society of Freemasonry; and the *trowel* is a symbol of the Mason's craft. (Much of the society's symbolism derives from the stonemason's trade.)

Freemasonry has been defined as "a peculiar system of morality veiled in allegory and illustrated by symbols"; and Swift frequently referred to symbols, as for example, he did above, or when he said he identified one location of treasure with "a symbol of a triangle"—one which is important in Freemasonry.[33]

Since the geological and historical evidence was against Swift having found great "veins" of silver in Eastern Kentucky, I began a study of texts on Freemasonry and glossaries of its terms. As a result, I noted a preponderance of seemingly Masonic expressions in the *Journal* which indeed appeared to have been "veiled in allegory and illustrated by symbols." According to *A New Encyclopedia of Freemasonry*, "the significance is in the allegory and not in any point of history which may lie behind it."[34]

And so I wrote in Kentucky's *Filson Club History Quarterly* (Oct. 1980):

As part of the allegory, Swift claims that—when he left the "richest mine" for the last time—he "walled it up with masonry form." Otherwise an unlikely expression, we need only capitalize "masonry" to see that this says, in effect, that the meaning has been concealed or "veiled" in Masonic fashion. It may be read with a knowing wink.[35]

Eventually, I traced the Swift legend to the year 1788—the year Freemasonry was founded in Kentucky. I further discovered that the scheming genius, John Filson—who had first reported on the tale and had even claimed to have found the mine—was then living in the home of a Master Mason. (The early records being lost, I was unable to prove that Filson had been a Mason; but Filson's biographer wrote to say that he believed I was right in suggesting Filson had created the allegory.)

The reader no doubt anticipates my budding hypothesis as to the explanation of the coffins mystery. But before returning to that mystery, let me make one other brief digression.

Freemasons have as one of their allegorical subjects a "secret vault."[36] Hence it was with great interest that in researching another treasure tale (of Virginia legend), I noted that the treasure had supposedly been desposited in a hidden "vault." A letter by the alleged depositor himself claimed that the treasure had been discovered "in a cleft of the rocks"— a specific Masonic expression which (as I learned) will cause one's Masonic friends to smile knowingly upon hearing it. I was amused at one pair of authors' conclusion that the protagonist may have been a Freemason. It seems not to have occurred to them—despite the lack of evidence that he ever existed—that both he and the story were fictitious. Eventually, circumstantial evidence suggested a suspect in the creation of this tale; and on inquiry I learned that this individual had indeed been a member of a Virginia Masonic lodge![37]

To return to the Barbados vault story, I did not at first connect it with the "secret vault" of Masonic allegory. Although the legend of the latter concerns King Solomon's subterranean depository of certain great secrets, and although the Masonic rites of the Master Mason degree feature a quest after such vague secrets (specifically "that which is lost," which, in the end, remain lost), I was not aware that the symbolism extended to a burial vault. But I learned that it does.

In a note to the "Select Master's Degree" of one Masonic text (with "foot note quotations from standard Masonic authors"), is this:

> The vault was, therefore, in the ancient mysteries, symbolic of the grave, for initiation was symbolic of death, where alone Divine Truth is to be found . . . . We significantly speak of the place of initiation as "the secret vault, where reign silence, secrecy and darkness." It is in this sense of an entrance through the grave into eternal life, that the Select Master is to view the recondite but beautiful symbolism of the secret vault. Like every other myth and allegory of Masonry, the historical

relation may be true or it may be false; it may be founded on fact or the invention of imagination; the lesson is still there, and the symbolism teaches it exclusive of the history.[38]

Also in the Mark Master's degree is considerable symbolism of the grave, including such statements as "the coffin is deposited in the grave," and "soon shall our bodies moulder to dust." And in Gertrude Jobes's *Dictionary of Mythology, Folklore and Symbols* we learn that "in Freemasonry" the coffin "symbolizes death and rebirth."[39]

We may now relate Masonic symbolism to the Barbados vault story. In Lucas's account, he states: "I examined the walls, the arch and every part of the vault and found every part old and similar; and a mason in my presence struck every part of the bottom with his hammer and all was solid."[40]

In the Royal Arch degree of Masonry—to which the "arch" above may have been in cryptic reference (just as the "vault" suggests the "secret vault" which, in Masonry, is said to have been "curiously arched")— there is a reference to the "sound of the hammer." According to Macoy's *Illustrated History and Cyclopedia of Freemasonry*, "The blow of the Master's hammer commands industry, silence, or the close of labour, and every brother respects or honors its sound."[41]

Furthermore, the above passage from Lucas very strongly echoes the statement from the Royal Arch degree, "We have examined the secret vault"! Indeed, in that very degree, the striking of stone—to see if it sounds hollow or solid—is the means by which the secret vault is sought for and finally located![42] Moreover, the word "solid" has special significance in Masonry. Macoy enters the term in his encyolopedia and quotes from an old lecture: ". . . A solid . . . is the whole system of divine laws, as existing in practice . . . For the length, breadth, and height of the whole law in practice must be perfect."[43]

Earlier in his account, Lucas had reported: "On the 7th of July 1819 private marks had been made at the mouth of the vault in the mason work; and on the 18th of April 1820 the vault was opened. . . ."[44] Here is a clear reference to the Mark Master's degree since "each Mason employed in building the Temple of Solomon [and hence Solomon's secret vault] was required to place a peculiar mark upon his work. . . ."[45] The ritual of the Mark Master's degree specifically uses the exact phrase employed by Lucas (and found in most of the earlier accounts as well) when it states that "every Mark Master Mason must place his own *private mark. . . .*" (my emphasis).[46] It is also suggestive that Lucas referred (above) to the cement—which in the Master Mason degree is "the cement which unites a building into one common mass"—as "mason work."[47]

A further example: Orderson says (in the Lucas manuscript) that in 1812 an infant's coffin "had been thrown from the north-east corner of the vault where it had been placed to the opposite angle."[48] Masonry derives much of its symbolism from geometry (hence the letter "G" in the insignia); and, of the three kinds of angles, Masonry employs "the right angle, or angle of 90 degrees, because it is the form of the trying square, an important working tool of Masonry, and *the symbol* of mortality" (my emphasis).[49] Orderson's "north-east corner" is a particular Masonic term. As Macoy informs, the corner-stone is "the principle and important stone in the foundation of an edifice. This stone is usually laid in the north-east corner, and unites two walls. . . . An important symbol in the Mark Master's degree."[50] And as A. G. Mackey states, the "north-east corner" is "an important ceremony of the first degree, which refers to the north-east corner of the lodge" and "is explained by the symbolism of the corner-stone."[51] I find it highly suggestive that the accounts name the *north-east* corner rather than the other three possibilities—which are not Masonically significant.

Why were the metal coffins restless, while the nonmetallic ones remained *in situ?* Probably because it is said in Masonry (see Duncan's *Ritual*, p. 268) that "he who wishes to be initiated into Free Masonry must be willing to relinquish all descriptions of metal. . . ."[52] And the suggestion (although rejected) of an inundation in the vault? "Inundations" is another Masonic concept entered in Macoy's *Cyclopedia.*[53]

Perhaps the reader suspects I am reading too much into the accounts, and might continue to suspect it even if I drew (as I easily could) numerous more distinctive parallels between the early accounts and Freemasonry. But let us leave off, for the moment, the interpreting of phrases and consider some other intriguing evidence—one piece of which concerns a curious error.

One of the early narratives has, for identification, become known as "A" (a designation supplied by folklorist Andrew Lang[54] and followed by Rupert Gould). On the back of one of the sketches of the coffins accompanying the "A" version was written "J. Anderson, Rector." Gould suggests this was "probably a mistake for 'T. Orderson,'" which is certainly quite plausible.[55] However, is it merely an unusual coincidence that J. Anderson (James Anderson, who, like Orderson, was a Doctor of Divinity) was one of the most important figures (for his celebrated *Constitutions,* 1723) in all of Freemasonry?[56] A suggestive error, that!

Another curiosity is found in the account of the Barbados vault legend by Sir Arthur Conan Doyle. As John Godwin observed:

> In what was probably the silliest magazine article he ever wrote, Sir Arthur declared that the turmoil was due to a substance called "effluvia." The effluvia was brought into the vault by the Negro slaves carrying the coffins. Now effluvium, in the dictionary sense, means simply exhalation [or noxious odor]. But Doyle, in a delightfully nebulous way, has the effluvia combine with certain unnamed "forces" inside the sealed vault. The combination then becomes a combustive force which proceeds to toss around the contents of the tomb. . . .
>
> Sir Arthur was modest enough to call this a "provisional theory." The great pipe-smoking sleuth he created would undoubtedly have called it something else.[57]

I too was struck by the strangeness of Conan Doyle's article,[58] all the more so by his postulating "effluvia" as an explanation of the mystery. That is a curious word, effluvium. But it is one well known to Masons since it appears in the Master Mason degree;[59] not only that, but it does so specifically in reference to "the grave"! If Conan Doyle were speaking Masonically tongue-in-cheek, then his explanation made sense after all; but it would surely have to mean that Doyle was a Freemason—to which possibility two knowledgeable Sherlockians expressed their doubts. However, Holmesean scholar John Bennett Shaw wrote me to say that, Yes, certainly, Conan Doyle had been a Mason, and he sent me published data on Doyle's membership.[60] (Several of the Holmes stories contain references to Freemasonry, and "The Musgrave Ritual" features a secret vault—with both hidden treasure and a corpse—plus such Masonic phrases as "cardinal points." Interestingly, another story contains passages that seem derived from the Barbados vault mystery: Holmes states at one point, "In that case we must work without you, Mr. Mason. You can show us the crypt and then leave us." Again, Watson narrates, "It was an hour or more before Holmes came to a leaden coffin standing on end before the entrance to the vault."[61])

Well, perhaps this is merely another coincidence. But then what about Robert Dale Owen's account of the restless coffins incident which allegedly took place at Arensburg, on the island of Oesel in the Baltic?

Owen's account is given in his 1869 *Footfalls on the Boundary of Another World;* and the disturbances related are, says Andrew Lang, in relation to those in Barbados, "*precisely* parallel." So very similar are the accounts that Lang suggests the possibility, without drawing the definite conclusion, that the alleged source of Owen's story (one Baron de Guldenstubbe—or Owen himself?) may have "plagiarized" the "whole story."[62]

Owen's tale does contain some imaginative details by way of improvement: Mysterious noises frightened some horses; wood ashes (instead of sand) were strewn to detect foot-marks; and (a grotesque touch) a shriveled arm was seen to protrude from one of the coffins![63]

The story is highly doubtful. The noted paranormal investigator Frank Podmore researched the tale, observing first of all that the story was third-hand; and that—although Owen claimed otherwise—there were no official documents attesting to the disturbances, neither in the archives of the Consistory of Oelsen, nor in those of the church, nor in any other place.[64]

Owen's narrative has some odd elements which seem Masonic in nature. For example, although the vault floor was of wood, he refers to it as "pavement"—a key Masonic term found in glossaries of the craft's symbolism.[65]

In the Royal Arch degree, the Principal Sojourner says, ". . . we . . . will make an alarm. . . ." Hence it is, perhaps, that Owen's account of the disturbances says that (on hearing noises issuing from the vault) some passersby "raised the alarm."[66]

Because of such touches, I thought it important to learn if Robert Dale Owen had been a Freemason and so queried the Masonic Lodge of New Harmony, Indiana, where he had once been a resident. The secretary replied: "Although Robert Dale Owen did not belong to [this lodge], I have been told by several people that he was a Freemason."[67]

While we are discussing the subject of plagiarism, it is worthwhile to mention a different possible source for the Barbados story. The *European Magazine* for September 1815 describes "The Curious Vault at Stanton in Suffolk" and briefly tells of coffins "displaced" on several occasions. It contains the speculation that the disturbances were "occasioned by water . . . though no sign of it appeared at the different periods of time that the vault was opened." This is a point also stressed by Nathan Lucas. Note that this account was published many years before any of the Barbados narratives were actually written down.[68] (The Orderson portion of the Lucas manuscript is dated 1824.) But did Lucas know of this published account? He did: He quoted from it![69]

Naturally, if the hypothesis I was beginning to form was valid— that the Barbados vault story was fictitious, specifically that it was a Masonic myth or allegory relating to the "secret vault"—then that would mean that Freemasons had been in Barbados by at least the time the first accounts were written. I posed the question to my Barbadian researcher, who soon learned that not only did Freemasonry exist there during the time period in question, but it had been established as early as 1740.[70]

I wondered: Had Lord Combermere himself been a Freemason? I was able to borrow copies of the two volumes of his posthumously published *Memoirs and Correspondence* (1866), compiled by his second (post-Barbados) wife, which I studied. I eventually discovered a reference to "the Masonic body, of which Lord Combermere had been for forty-five years the Provincial Grand-Master in Cheshire."[71] Since he would certainly have been a Mason for some time before becoming a Grand-Master, it seems a virtual certainty (considering that he died in 1865) that Combermere was a Mason during the period of the alleged disturbances in which he figures so prominently. (At least, subtracting 45 years from 1865, he would have been a Grand-Master in 1820, the year of the final reported disturbance.) The account of the coffins story in the *Memoirs* is most interesting. Certainly it is colorful enough. One problem, however, is that Combermere did not write it; indeed there is no evidence that he himself ever wrote anything about the alleged incidents. The *Memoirs* account was taken, says Gould, from a pamphlet titled *Death's Deeds,* published anonymously in London in 1860, and with its introduction signed merely "K.R." But the anonymous "K.R." asserts that the account "has been corroborated directly to myself by the venerable Lord Combermere."[72]

Be that as it may (and it should be noted that several details are not supported by the earliest versions), the comparatively lengthy account in the *Memoirs* is perhaps the most Masonic in symbolism of all the narratives. "Masons" are of course much in evidence, as are the telling "private marks" and other elements. When the vault was last opened, and the "masons," the *Memoirs* account says, "endeavoured to remove the stone it resisted with unwonted weight. Increased force was applied, but still it remained *immovable"* (my emphasis). Interestingly, the concept of movability and immovability, including the symbolism of the "immovable" stone (known as the "rough ashlar," a hewn stone), figures prominently in Masonic symbolism.[73]

There is also an emphasis on darkness-to-light symbolism in the *Memoirs* narrative. For instance, when the vault was opened, "nothing was distinctly visible in the darkness of its buried night. Still, the light which entered through the narrow crevice seemed to cut across some black object close to the portal, so near that the thread-like ray lay brightly visible, prevented by this massive black substance [a coffin] from dispersing itself into the reigning darkness within."[74]

Now, in Masonry—which is termed the "Great Light"—light symbolizes enlightenment. The concept is expressed as *lux e tenebris* or "light out of darkness." And in the Royal Arch degree, it is stated that among the duties of the Principal Sojourner are "to make darkness light before them, and crooked things [such as mis-aligned coffins?] straight." A. G. Mackey adds that light is also "the symbol of the autopsy."[75] Note how the passage from the *Memoirs* (quoted above) parallels this one from the Royal Arch degree: "Most Excellent, in pursuance of your orders, we repaired to the secret vault, and let down one of our companions. The sun at this time was at its meridian height, the rays of which enabled him to discover a small box or chest, standing on a pedestal, curiously wrought. . . . On discovering it, he involuntarily found his hand raised in this position (giving the sign as shown . . .), to guard his eyes from the intense light and best reflected from it."[76]

The Combermere account adds a new element, the "questioning" of "the masons" which was done "very closely." It is significant that the ritual questioning of Freemasons is important in many of the degrees, as for example:[77]

Q. How were you received in a chapter of Royal Arch Masons?
A. Under a living arch.
Q. Why under a living arch?
A. To imprint upon my mind. . . [etc.].
Q. How were you then disposed of?
A. We were conducted. . .[etc].
Q. [Etc., etc.]

Following the discovery that Combermere had indeed been a Mason, I sought to learn if others connected with the story had also been members of the Fraternity.

With the help of Mr. Foster of the Department of Tourism, I made contact with a Masonic authority in Barbados. I had not stated to anyone my specific suspicions, but this individual must have guessed, for he (quite uncharacteristically of other Masons of my experience) refused to divulge any information on early memberships until I had written him in detail as to my intentions. Since I have made several such inquiries, and have always received the desired information courteously (indeed, lists of Masonic members are frequently published proudly in various local histories), I was taken aback by his response.

I replied rather vaguely that I simply was interested in whether "masons" in the early accounts might have referred to Masons, as a detail perhaps of historic interest. He did indicate that he had material of use to me, but it was not forthcoming. Instead, there was a long delay, another query from me, an excuse in reply, and then another lengthy and (despite my queries) final silence. After many months I was told he had moved from the island.[78]

My researcher was informed later by "a prominent member of the organization" that "there are no records of members." I urged her to pursue the matter independently and she eventually uncovered the fact that Sir R. Boucher Clark (one of the alleged eyewitnesses to the events) had been a Past Master of one of the lodges.[79]

All the foregoing evidence had persuaded me that my "Masonic hypothesis" was probably correct, but there was yet a further piece of evidence—one that would seem quite stunningly to confirm my hypothesis. Another instance of restless coffins, also in Barbados, transpired in 1943. This time it was specifically *a party of Freemasons* who made the visit to the vault! And this vault, in the churchyard of St. Michael's Cathedral in Bridgetown, was that of *the founder of Freemasonry in Barbados* (Alexander Irvine) and of *another prominent Mason* (the former governor, Sir Evan MacGregor)!

As the story is told by Aspinall in the *Journal of the Barbados Museum and Historical Society,* the stone slabs were removed from the steps and the "arched doorway" was revealed:

> Then brick by brick the wall was taken down. After a few bricks had been removed the opening disclosed some metal object resting against the inner side; then after more had been shifted it was seen that it

was the end of a large leaden coffin one end of which was propped up against the wall, while the other rested on the floor. After the removal of the last row of bricks the coffin came to rest on the floor of the vault, lying, not parallel to the sides, but askew. It was the only coffin in the vault and the inscription upon it proved it was that of Sir Evan MacGregor. . . . Of Irvine's coffin there was not the slightest trace and the visitors came to the conclusion that it must have been made of wood and have fallen to pieces when the Governor was interred. But at the far end of the vault, on a stone ledge running the entire length of the vault, were a skull and some bones—apparently all that was left of Alexander Irvine.

Aspinall adds that "As was the case at Christ Church, there was not the slightest indication that floods or an earthquake were responsible for the derangement."[80]

The image of skull-and-bones reposing on a ledge strikes me as a literary one; and it seems particularly so in light of Masonic symbolism and allegory. It obviously suggests Masonic "relics" which are "personal memorials of those among the dead who have been distinguished during life by eminent qualities" (such as Irvine and MacGregor).[81] In fact, in the Knights Templar degree, the Eminent Commander says, "Pilgrim, you here behold an emblem of mortality" which is a "skull and cross bones" and which reminds one of "the gloomy hour of dissolution."[82] Several other similarities to the original vault legend will be obvious.

In summary, it seems that no naturalistic cause can explain the Chase Vault mystery, and there are reasons to doubt the actual fact of the occurrences. The story may have been suggested by one from England and in turn may have served as a model for a similar tale set in the Baltic.

Much evidence—e.g. references to "masons," "private marks" and so forth—suggests that the story was shaped into an allegory relating to the "secret vault" of Freemasonry. At least two of those who figured in the alleged incidents were important Masons, and others may well have been.

And then there is the 1943 vault story which specifically mentions Freemasons at a Masons' vault.

These details bring—as Masons would say—some light out of the darkness, and, taken together, seem clearly to lead us to what in Freemasonry is termed "the Conclusion of the Whole Matter."

Select Bibliography

Aspinall, Algernon. "An Unsolved Barbados Mystery." *Journal of the Barbados Museum and Historical Society* 13 (1945):126-131. An article relating a second "restless coffins" incident in Barbados, which supposedly transpired in 1943; provides interesting parallels and—because of the involvement of Freemasons—insights into the Chase Vault mystery.

Gould, Rupert T. *Oddities,* 23-51. 1928. Reprint. New Hyde Park, N.Y.: University Books, 1966. An account of the Chase Vault ("restless coffins") mystery of Barbados; a standard work on the subject.

"The Lucas Manuscript Volumes." *Journal of the Barbados Museum and Historical Society* 12, no. 3 (May 1945):57. An alleged firsthand account of the last opening of the Chase Vault, from the manuscript of Nathan Lucas.

Macoy, Robert. *Illustrated History and Cyclopedia of Freemasonry.* New York: Macoy, 1908. One of many reference works containing data on symbolism and allegory in Freemasonry (useful in discussing the Chase Vault Mystery from a Masonic viewpoint).

Acknowledgments

For copies of early accounts of the Barbados coffins story and for other historical material—often in books designated "rare"—thanks are due the Bridgetown, Barbados, Public Library; the Barbados Museum and Historical Society; Barbados Department of Archives; Van Pelt Library, University of Pennsylvania; Library Company of Philadelphia; and the Inter-Library Loan Departments of the University of Kentucky (to whose Barbara Hale is due special thanks) and the Lexington, Kentucky, Public Library.

We are particularly grateful to the editors of *Fate* magazine—in which this material first appeared (in the April and May issues of 1985)—for permission to reprint it.

11. FIERY FATE
Specter of
"Spontaneous Human Combustion"

Have you any theory, Holmes?

—DR. WATSON
"The Adventure of Shoscombe Old Place"

If the fiery death of Mary Reeser was not actually due to "spontaneous human combustion" (SHC)—a phenomenon science says does not exist—then what was the nature of a fire that could cause so little damage to anything else in her apartment yet so completely consume her body that there remained only ashes, a few bones, and an eerie shrunken skull?

The mystery began on July 2, 1951, in St. Petersburg, Florida. At eight o'clock that Monday morning, a telegram which had arrived for the sixty-seven-year-old widow was signed for by her landlady, Mrs. Pansy Carpenter. Mrs. Carpenter then walked toward Mrs. Reeser's apartment at the opposite end of the four-unit building.

But when she attempted to open a hallway door and found the knob too hot to grasp, she cried for help. Two house painters responded, running from across the street. Albert Delnet—followed by his co-worker,

---

Investigated with John F. Fischer.

L. P. Clements, and Mrs. Carpenter—advanced through the smoke-filled hallway into Mrs. Reeser's efficiency apartment.

Inside they found a burning beam above a partition, and nearby discovered the gruesome remains of a woman—most notably a slippered foot, burned off at the ankle. Amid the heap of ashes were coiled springs from the big armchair in which the woman had perished.

Investigators arriving on the scene noted additional details. Soot had blackened the ceiling and walls above an almost level line some three and a half feet above the floor. There was negligible heat damage below the smoke line, but above it plastic electric switches had melted, along with a plastic tumbler in the bathroom and some candles on a dresser. An electric clock, which still worked when plugged into another outlet, had stopped at 4:20.

As the investigators tried to determine what had happened to Mrs. Reeser, and as wire services sent news of the "cinder woman mystery" across the country, theorists deluged officials with letters and telegrams offering solutions. One held that the elderly widow had been murdered by "a fiend with a blow torch," another that she had swallowed some explosive material and had "blown herself up." Still another said, "A ball of fire came through the window and hit her. I seen it happen."[1] And then the specter of SHC came on the scene. As the June 6 issue of the *Atlanta Constitution* reported (under the wry headline, "How Woman Was Incinerated Stumps All But Amateurs"): "An amateur physiologist said his studies indicate that 'spontaneous internal combustion' was possible. He said sudden rare cross-mixture of chemicals in the body might cause this."[2] Might more recent SHC proponents be correct in suggesting that SHC is related to "geomagnetic fluctuations"[3] or to man's "electrodynamic being?"[4]

What of the possibility of an analogous phenomenon, "preternatural combustibility" (or PC)—an imagined condition in which "the cells reach the critical stage of ignition but need a spark from an outside source before they will burst into flame."[5]

To answer such questions, we launched a two-year investigation that focused on Mrs. Reeser's death but began with a historical overview of the controversy over SHC/PC. Our lengthy, two-part report was published in the journal of the International Association of Arson Investigators.[6]

We found a widely publicized mid-nineteenth-century debate over the phenomenon that is typical of the continuing controversy. That debate was sparked (so to speak) by Charles Dickens's novel *Bleak House* wherein a sinister, drunken Mr. Krook perished by "spontaneous combustion." Response came from George Henry Lewes, the philosopher and critic, who publicly accused Dickens of perpetuating a vulgar superstition. Lewes insisted that such a death was a scientific impossibility,[7] a view shared by the great scientist Liebig, who wrote: "The opinion that a man can burn of himself is not founded on a knowledge of the circumstances of the death, but on the reverse of knowledge—on complete ignorance of all the causes or conditions which preceded the accident and caused it."[8]

Thus rationalists like Lewes were seizing the scientific high ground with the question of *cause;* Dickens on the other hand was arguing primarily from *effect:* He cited several cases of the phenomenon, some of which had been attested to by medical men of the time. To assess these contrary views we researched thirty seemingly representative cases that spanned more than two and a half centuries (see Appendix).

One of the earliest reported cases took place in February of 1725, at Rheims, when the burned remains of a Madame Millet were found upon her kitchen floor, a portion of which had also burned. Although her husband was convicted of murdering her, a higher court reversed the decision, attributing the death to spontaneous combustion. Actually, the woman was one who "got intoxicated every day," had gone to the kitchen "to warm herself," and was discovered only "a foot and a half's distance" from the hearth. Therefore, Thomas Stevenson, in his 1883 treatise on medical jurisprudence, suggested that her clothes had "accidentally ignited."[9]

In contrast is another early case, the 1731 death of the Countess Bandi of Cesena, Italy, aged sixty-two, who was *not* given to intoxication. Although her body was supposedly reduced to "a heap of ashes," part of the head remained, and the legs and arms were not burned. The ashes contained "a greasy and stinking moisture," soot floated in the air, and from the window there "trickled down a greasy, loathsome, yellowish liquor with an unusual stink." However, the case—which served as one of Dickens's sources—seems quite explicable when further data is added: On the floor was an empty, ash-covered lamp on which the countess had apparently fallen, its burning oil no doubt aiding in the immolation.[10]

At least three other eighteenth-century cases involved women who drank: Grace Pett of Ipswich, who perished in 1744, her burned remains attended by a fatty stain and lying near both a fireplace and a fallen candle;[11] a Frenchwoman, Madame De Boiseon, aged eighty in 1749, who supposedly "drank nothing but spirits for several years" and whose body was still burning in a chair placed "before the fire";[12] and, sometime prior to 1774, fifty-two-year-old Mary Clues of Coventry who was "much given to drinking" and whose death a medical investigator attributed to her shift having caught fire, either from "the candle on the chair or a coal falling from the grate."[13]

Sometime before 1835 (when Beck published the case in his *Elements of Medical Jurisprudence*) an intoxicated, thirty-year-old Hannah Bradshaw burned to death in New York. A four-foot hole had burned through the floor of her room, and her bones and a burned-off foot were found on the ground underneath. Significantly, a candlestick, with a portion of candle in it, was found near the edge of the hole.[14]

Other nineteenth-century cases include the 1852 death of John Anderson, a wood hauler and "notorious dram drinker," who was seen to get down from his cart, stumble and burn to death. His body was only *charred,* which is consistent with his clothes having caught fire and with there being no additional fuel source. Anderson's lighted pipe was found under his body.[15]

In 1870, in France, the body of a drunken woman was found on her smoldering bedroom floor. There was considerable damage to the torso, with a "greasy black soot adhering to the vertebrae." Although there was "no fire in the grate"—at least none remaining—the body nevertheless lay partially *across the hearth* and the drunken woman may have set her clothes ablaze while attempting to light the fire.[16]

After the turn of the century, in 1908, a retired English schoolmarm named Wilhelmina Dewar was found dead—her body burned, but the bed on which it was lying remaining unscorched. Under questioning at an inquest, however, her sister confessed she had actually discovered Wilhelmina "burned, but still alive," and had "helped her walk to the bed where she had died."[17]

From the above cases (typical of the thirty we researched), some patterns emerge. For example, we noted that there did seem to be some correlation between drunkenness and instances of SHC. Early theorists, including members of the temperance movement, had suggested that alcohol-impregnated tissues were rendered highly combustible, but scientists had refuted the notion by experimentation and had pointed out that a person would die of alcohol poisoning long before imbibing enough alcohol to have even a slight effect on the body's flammability.[18] We determined instead that the correlation was likely due to drunken persons being more careless with fire and less able to properly respond to an accident.

We also found an even more significant correlation: In those instances in which the destruction of the body was relatively minimal, the only significant fuel source seems to have been the individual's clothes, but where the destruction was considerable, additional fuel sources—chair stuffing, wooden flooring, floor coverings, etc.—augmented the combustion. Materials under the body appear also to have helped retain melted fat which flowed from the body and then volatilized and burned, destroying more of the body and yielding still more liquified fat to continue the process known as "the candle effect."[19] (In one case, Stevenson explained that a hempen mat had become so combustible due to "the melted human fat with which it was impregnated," that it "burnt like a link"—i.e., like a pitch torch.[20]

Such correlation of the amount of destruction with the utilization of available fuel sources makes a forceful argument against the notion of "preternatural combustibility." And the presence of plausible sources of the ignition—proximate candles, lamps, fireplaces—makes the postulation of "spontaneous human combustion" completely unwarranted (see Figure 18).

Proponents of SHC argue that bodies are difficult to burn because of the great amounts of water they contain; but the water is boiled off ahead of the advancing fire.[21] Again, they argue from comparisons to the destructive force of crematories, asserting for instance that a temperature of 2,500 or more degrees Fahrenheit is required to destroy a body in three hours.[22]

Actually, an authoritative forensic source states that only a one-and-a-half hour period is required at 1600-1800 degrees.[23] In any case, if a longer time is involved, a lower temperature is required. As D. J. X. Halliday of the Fire Investigation Unit of London's Metropolitan Police Forensic Science Laboratory explains, "Cremation is intended to destroy a body in the shortest possible time and is therefore carried out under extreme conditions, but a relatively small fire can consume flesh and calcine bone if it is allowed to burn for a long time."[24] And many hours

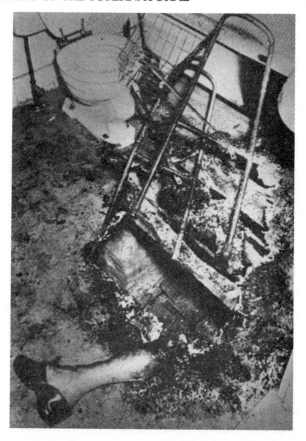

Figure 18. The gruesome remains of Dr. J. Irving Bentley, whose death in Pennsylvania in 1966 is frequently attributed to "SHC." Actually, the ninety-two-year-old pipe-smoking physician frequently dropped ashes on his clothes—as burns on the bedroom rug indicated he had done a final time. He made his way with his walker to the bathroom in a vain attempt to extinguish the flames. The fact that he shed his robe, found smoldering in the bathtub, demonstrates an external rather than internal source of ignition.

were typically involved in the cases we researched wherein the destruction was extensive.

But what of a case in which there was no known cause for the ignition, and the body was almost completely destroyed—except for a foot and "shrunken skull"—yet the surroundings were relatively undamaged? That is the way the celebrated "cinder woman mystery"—termed "probably the best-documented modern case" of SHC[25]—is sometimes portrayed. But our re-investigation of that case—which involved digging up the police report, death certificate, and contemporary news accounts—provides a lesson in the need to treat instances of alleged SHC on a case-by-case basis.

For example, one account[26] neglects to include the essential facts that when last seen Mrs. Reeser was wearing a flammable nightdress and housecoat, sitting in the overstuffed chair in which she subsequently died, and smoking a cigarette. Also omitted was the fact that she had told her son, a physician, that she had taken two sleeping pills and intended to take two more before retiring.[27]

Other accounts, while conceding that Mrs. Reeser may indeed have died as a result of dropping her cigarette as she dozed off and that SHC may not have been the cause, nevertheless postulate that the concept of "preternatural combustibility" is still feasible. Vincent Gaddis scoffs: "That flames from a nightgown, housecoat, and a chair that doesn't flare up but smolders, could create sufficient heat to cremate a large human body is ridiculous. And the notion that fluid-saturated fatty tissues, ignited by an outside flame, will burn and produce enough heat to destroy the rest of the body is nonsense."[28]

Gaddis was reacting to the conclusion stated in the official police report (the text of which is given in one source[29]) that "Once the body became ignited, almost complete destruction occurred from the destruction of its own fatty tissues." In fact, we learned that Mrs. Reeser was a "plump" woman and that a quantity of "grease"—obviously residue from her body—was left at the spot where the chair had stood.

As to Gaddis's insistence that the chair would not burn, Thomas J. Ohlemiller—an expert in smoldering combustion at the Center for Fire Research, Department of Commerce—told us: "Fire deaths caused by cigarette ignition of bedding and upholstery are among the most common in the U.S. . . . The smoldering spreads slowly and can sometimes consume the entire piece of furniture with no flames." Ohlemiller added, "More commonly the smoldering process abruptly ignites the gases coming from the object; this may occur an hour or more after the smoldering process was initiated."[30]

In the Reeser case, what probably happened is that the chair's stuffing burned slowly, fueled by the melted body fat and aided by partially open windows. From the time the widow was last seen sitting in the chair until her remains were discovered, almost twelve hours had elapsed.

Gaddis had further questioned why—if the fatty tissue had indeed burned—it did not spread the fire. The answer is that, first of all, the fire did spread more than some accounts acknowledge: An adjacent end-table and lamp were destroyed and a ceiling beam had to be extinguished when firemen arrived. Besides, the melted fat would have been slowly absorbed by the chair's stuffing, and in any event the floor was of concrete.[31]

That one of the widow's feet remained entire may have been due to the fact that Mrs. Reeser had a stiff leg which she extended when sitting.[32] Or, as the burning chair collapsed and the body rolled out onto its right side, the foot reached beyond the radius of the fire.

One of the strangest and most frequently reported elements of the case—the alleged shrinking of the skull—probably never happened. The self-described "bone detective" who is often quoted on the subject merely referred to secondhand news accounts and thus spoke of "a roundish object identitfied as the head ."[33] Actually, as a forensic anthropologist theorized at our request, Mrs. Reeser's skull probably burst in the fire and was destroyed, and the "roundish object" could have been merely "a globular lump that can result from the musculature of the neck where it attaches to the base of the skull."[34]

In conclusion, what has been described as "probably the best-documented modern case" of "spontaneous human combustion" is actually attributable to the deadly combination of cigarette, flammable night-clothes, and sleeping pills. And the notion of "preternatural combustibity" must yield to the evidence supporting the "candle effect"—one in which a body's fat liquefies and participates in its own destruction.

Although even a lean body contains a significant amount of fat (present even in the bone marrow),[35] other factors may be involved in a given instance, and we therefore urge investigation of cases on their own evidence. The operative word is *investigation,* not merely debunking—although the former may surely result in the latter in instances of alleged "spontaneous human combustion."

Select Bibliography

Allen, W. S. "Weird Cremation." *True Detective,* December 1951, 42-45, 93-94. A valuable early report on the fiery death of Mary Reeser.

Arnold, Larry E. "The Flaming Fate of Dr. John Irving Bentley." *Pursuit,* Fall 1976, 75-79. An account of the 1966 Bentley case by an arch-promoter of the alleged phenomenon of spontaneous human combustion.

————. "Human Fireballs." *Science Digest,* October 1981, 88-91, 115. An absurd attempt to link "spontaneous human combustion" with "geomagnetic fluctuations."

Blizin, Jerry. "The Reeser Case." *St. Petersburg Times* (Florida), 9 August 1951. An article with the text of the official police report offering an explanation for the death of Mary Reeser.

Gadd, Laurence D., and the editors of the World Almanac. *The Second Book of the Strange,* 33-36. New York: World Almanac, 1981. A version of the Reeser case that omits essential details, such as Mrs. Reeser's cigarette and the fact that she had taken sleeping pills.

Gaddis, Vincent H. *Mysterious Fires and Lights.* New York: David McKay, 1967. An argument for the existence of "SHC" in the context of a stubbornly credulous presentation of fire-related mysteries.

Gee, D. J. "A Case of 'Spontaneous Combustion.' " *Medicine, Science and the Law* 5 (1965):37-38. A report on experiments relative to the so-called candle effect—a process which may help explain the severe destruction of the body in some instances of supposedly "spontaneous" fire deaths.

Liebig, Justus von. *Familiar Letters on Chemistry,* letter no. 22. London: Taylor, Walton & Maberly, 1851. Arguments against the alleged phenomenon of "spontaneous human combustion" by the great nineteenth-century scientist.

Acknowledgments

In addition to individuals cited in the text or in the references, we wish to thank the staff of the Margaret I. King Library, University of Kentucky, for repeated assistance in obtaining needed publications.

Material in this chapter (and Appendix) first appeared in *The Fire and Arson Investigator* (March and June issues, 1984). It was later abridged for articles in *Fate* (April 1985) and the *Skeptical Inquirer* (Summer 1987).

12. AFTERWORD
Some Parting Shots

It is a capital mistake to theorize before one has data. Insensibly one begins to twist facts to suit theories, instead of theories to suit facts.

—SHERLOCK HOLMES
"A Scandal in Bohemia"

These cases have represented only a sampling of claims of "supernatural" phenomena—or phenomena, at least, that supposedly defied science's ability to explain them. From one perspective the results are entirely disappointing, since the casualty rate approximates 100 percent. There is much to be learned, however, from such negative findings.

A crucial lesson is the necessity of guarding against deception. This includes deception by outright liars and hoaxers, by the deluded, and by writers who range from the merely negligent to the cynically manipulative. And it also includes self-deception, a too-willing acceptance of fanciful claims—even, on occasion, a stubborn refusal to heed clear danger signals, in which case the term *gullible* is appropriate.[1] An antidote to deception is to recall the maxim that "extraordinary claims require extraordinary proof," and, for self-deception, to consider the thesis that gullibility is fostered by want and to analyze one's motives accordingly.

Another lesson is for the confirmed skeptic, who is urged to test even that which tallies with his or her expectations. (Recall, for example, the appealing—but wrong—flooded-vault hypothesis for the Barbados coffins mystery.) In other words, a wise investigator will be skeptical even of his own skepticism.

We would also caution against extrapolating too much from the few examples herein. They do not represent proof against all "supernatural" occurrences (although they do reinforce the skeptical position). Rather, even though it may sometimes be useful to generalize, the unique nature of some of the solutions urges that we investigate mysteries on a case-by-case basis. Not all "spontaneous human combustion" victims are obese smokers who have taken sleeping pills, for example, nor are all "miraculous" images paintings.

A case-by-case approach invites the preparation of an individualized investigative strategy, devised to meet the particular needs of the matter at hand. In the case of the "two Will Wests," for instance, when blood samples were not available, genetic evidence was sought from fingerprint patterns and other sources.[2] In the various investigations in this casebook we have employed a wide range of additional techniques, including microchemical analyses, interviews of witnesses, controlled tests of persons claiming special powers, site inspections, historical research, physical experiments, folkloristic and iconographic studies, instrumental analyses, and more.

We were assisted by specialists in such diverse fields as archaeology, smoldering combustion, forensic identification, genetics, photography, engineering, pathology, art, genealogy, and additional fields, and we were also aided by other investigators, researchers, librarians, police officials, records clerks, and many, many others. We are grateful for their specific professional help as well as for their spirit of involvement. This often seems lacking in some scholars and scientists, who apparently feel that certain concerns are too "popular" and are thus beneath their elite status.

As for us, we remain involved. We know that a large percentage of people are not only intrigued by preternatural phenomena but believe that they have experienced them firsthand. So profound are the implications of these popularly perceived experiences, that the question is not *whether* such phenomena will be investigated, but *how*. It is with that in mind that we turn to an already increasing case load.

APPENDIX
Thirty Cases of
"Spontaneous Human Combustion"

From a surprisingly large number of cases of alleged SHC, we have selected thirty which we here present in abstract form. They are numbered for convenience, presented in chronological order, and accompanied by source citations. Following them is a brief commentary.

(1) February 1725: The wife of a man named Millet, of Rheims. Her burned remains—a portion of the head, a few vertebrae, and the lower extremities— were found upon the kitchen floor, a portion of which had also been burned. Her husband was convicted of murdering her; the motive is alleged to have been "an intrigue with a female servant." He was freed, however, after a higher court decided this was a case of spontaneous combustion. But neither assumption is necessary since the wife reportedly "got intoxicated every day" and was last seen when, unable to sleep, she went to the kitchen "to warm herself." Her remains were found only "a foot and a half's distance" from the fire on the kitchen hearth. Stevenson suggested that her clothes had been "accidentally ignited." (Beck 1835; Lewes 1961; Stevenson 1883)

    (2) 1731: The Countess Cornelia Bandi (or Baudi) of Cesena, Italy, aged 62 and *not* given to intoxication. Her body was reportedly reduced to "a heap of ashes" although the legs and arms were untouched. The head lay between the legs; burned away were the brain, part of the cranium, and the entire chin. When the ashes were touched they "left in the hand a greasy and stinking

moisture." Soot floated in the air of the room, "and from the lower part of the window, trickled down a greasy, loathsome, yellowish liquor with an unusual stink." *On the floor* was a lamp, empty of oil and covered with ashes, suggesting that the countess had fallen on the lamp, the flaming oil aiding in the immolation. *(Gentlemen's Magazine* 1746)

(3) April 1744: Grace Pett (or Kett, or Pitt), the 60-year-old wife of a fishmonger of the parish of St. Clement, Ipswich. Her burning body was found by her daughter, who extinguished the fire with water. Mrs. Pett reportedly had drunk "a large quantity of spirituous liquor," and was in the habit of leaving her bedroom, dressed in a cotton gown, to smoke a pipe. The trunk of the body "was in some measure incinerated, and resembled a heap of coals covered with white ashes." The extremities "had also participated in the burning," and a fatty stain was reported. She was found lying "with her head near the grate" in which it was said there was no fire (or at least none remaining). Close to her was a candle which "had burnt entirely out in the socket of the candle-stick." Her clothes may have ignited as she attempted to light the fire or as she smoked her pipe or brushed against the candle (which appears to have been knocked over). *(Annual Register* 1763; Beck 1835)

(4) 1749: Madame De Boiseon, a French woman, 80 years of age. She supposedly "drank nothing but spirits for several years." Her waiting-maid found her just as she had left her shortly before, seated in a chair, but with her body now burning. The maid gave the alarm and one of those responding attempted to extinguish the flames with his hand: "But they adhered to it, as if it had been dipped in brandy, or oil on fire." When water was poured on the body it seemed to burn even more violently "and was not extinguished till the whole flesh had been consumed" and "one leg only, and the two hands detached themselves from the rest of the bones." Beck mentioned the possibility of the woman's clothes having ignited; indeed, her chair had been placed "before the fire." (Beck 1835)

(5) Sometime before 1774 (when an account of the case was published): Mary Clues of Coventry, aged 52. She was "much given to drinking" and on at least one earlier occasion had fallen from bed, lying helpless until a neighbor happened by. She was found burned to death one morning in the bedroom of her ground-floor apartment, the walls of which were plaster and the floor of brick. Her body was largely destroyed, and the bones calcined. Found were the skull and spine along with the legs, and one thigh that had remained untouched. The medical man who investigated the death observed that the walls and everything in the room had been "coloured black." He supposed that her shift had caught fire, either from "the candle on the chair or a coal falling from the grate." (Lewes 1861)

(6) March 1802: An elderly Massachusetts woman. Her remains were found in the midst of a fire burning the wooden floor *near the hearth.* The fire had

to be extinguished. On the hearth and the contiguous flooring were found "a sort of greasy soot and ashes," and there was an "unusual" odor in the room. The evidence strongly suggests that the woman's clothes—which were completely consumed—had been set ablaze by the fire in the fireplace, and that her burning clothes ignited the floor which, in turn, served as fuel for the cremation. (Beck 1835)

(7) Recorded in the *Methodist Magazine* for 1809: About two o'clock one morning, the keeper of an almshouse in Limerick was called to the apartment of a man, where he found the body of a Mrs. Peacock "burning with fire and red as copper." The conflagration had begun in the loft above, which was still burning (presumably having to be extinguished), and the body had dropped through a large hole burned through the ceiling. In the upper room, in the grate, were the smoldering remains of a fire, "raked in the ashes, as is the manner of preserving fire by night." Possibly, while raking the coals, Mrs. Peacock had accidentally set her clothes afire, the burning wood underneath her fallen body apparently acting as a pyre. (Lewes 1861)

(8) Before 1835 (when it was published in Beck's *Elements of Medical Jurisprudence)*: An intoxicated, 30-year-old woman, Hannah Bradshaw, whose death was reported by a W. Dunlop of New York. In the middle of the woman's room, a hole of about four feet in diameter was burnt through the floor. The bones were found on the ground, about a foot below. Among the remains were most or all of the bones, and an intact right foot burned off near the ankle. Some flesh remained on the skull and on one shoulder, and the bowels were unconsumed. That portion of a chair within compass of the hole was burned. At the edge of the hole was found a part of the head and near it, a candlestick with a portion of a candle in it. Apparently the drunken woman had set her clothes afire with the candle. (Lewes 1861)

(9) Published in 1847: A 71-year-old Frenchman found lying in bed "in a state of combustion," his clothes and the bed coverings "almost entirely consumed; but the wood was only partially burnt." When his wife and son were suspected of murder, the body was exhumed and examined; spontaneous combustion was suggested; and the pair was acquitted. The man was "not fat, nor was he addicted to drunkenness," but "he had had a hot brick placed at his feet when he went to bed the preceding evening." Possibly, a cinder adhering to the heated brick had ignited the bedding. (Stevenson 1883)

(10) June 1847: The Countess of Goerlitz. Her body was discovered, burned but not burning, although some furniture and a portion of the floor were actually blazing and had to be extinguished. The body was badly burned, especially the head, which was "a nearly shapeless black mass," although a slipper was undamaged. Some "dark greasy matter" was observed. On investigation, a servant named Stauff was discovered to have the countess's jewels in his possession. He subsequently confessed that he had strangled the

countess after she surprised him in the act of robbery. In an attempt to conceal his crime, he had set the fire. (Lewes 1861; Stevenson 1883)

(11) Before 1852 (when it was reported by M. Devergie): A washer-woman, Marie Jeanne Antoinette Bally, aged 50. She had returned to her lodging one December evening in a state of drunkenness. Her exceedingly tiny room held no bed but only a chair, a chest, and curtains. At eight o'clock the following morning her remains were discovered along with those of the chair upon which she must have sat. The face, hair, neck, and upper portion of the shoulders "were not injured." However, the skin and muscles of the back, as well as the sides and anterior portion of the trunk, "were burnt." Of the arms, only the bones remained. The legs were burned only above the stockings. There was no fire in the fireplace, but underneath her was found "an earthen pot such as is used by the poor to hold a few coals to warm their feet." (Adelson 1952).

(12) July 1852: John Anderson, who carted wood from the forest of Darnaway, aged about 50 and "a notorious dram-drinker." A herd-boy, about a quarter of a mile away, reportedly saw him get down from his cart, stumble, and fall by the roadside. The boy found the body burning and extinguished the fire with several pails of water. Lewes observes that the body was only *"charred*—that is, burned, as it always is superficially when the clothes take fire." The drunken man's lighted pipe was found *under* his body. (Lewes 1861)

(13) Published in 1854 in England: A woman found dead in her room, her body still smoldering and the flesh burnt off the bones from the groin downward. A portion of the floor under the legs had burned and the leg bones had actually fallen through the hole, "leaving the feet unburnt on the floor." Subsequently a man who had been in the house at the time was arrested and he confessed to murdering the woman. Noting that the evidence suggested that the burning had occurred in the relatively short span of two hours, Stevenson explained "that the clothes of the deceased were much burnt, and that beneath the body there was a hempen mat, so combustible, owing to the melted human fat with which it was impregnated, that when ignited it burnt like a link" (i.e., a pitch torch). (Stevenson 1883)

(14) 1860: A Mrs. Pulley, whose body was found with the head lying on the hearth of her room. From the shoulders downward the oak floor had been burned through and "parts of her clothing and body had been destroyed by fire." The legs were undamaged. According to Stevenson, while there was no fire in the grate, "a brass candlestick was lying between the left arm and the body, the top of the candlestick being inclined toward it." He adds that "a proper inquiry" revealed "that it was a deliberate murder by strangulation," the killer having supposedly set fire to the body in an attempt to conceal his crime. (Stevenson 1883)

(15) Before 1861 (when the case was related by Lewes, citing Apjohn in

Cyclopaedia of Practical Medicine): A woman, referred to only as A.B., aged about 60. She and her daughter had retired to bed, "both being, as was their constant habit, in a state of intoxication." Before daybreak family members were alerted by smoke and discovered the woman's body, smoldering and "black as coal." The fire was extinguished "with difficulty." Although it was reported that the combustion did not "extend to the bedclothes," Lewes complained of the account: "No mention is made of the position of the body; we are not told whether it was on the floor, at some distance from the bed, or in the bed." Lewes also complained of the "silence" as to whether there might have been a lighted candle or other means of setting afire the woman's nightdress, which had indeed burned. (Lewes 1861)

(16) 1864: An unnamed woman whose death was reported by Stevenson in *The Principles and Practice of Medical Jurisprudence*. She was discovered in her room, which was filled with a "thick black offensive smoke." According to Stevenson, "Her clothes were on fire, and a chair had been burnt." Some of the flesh had been burned from the bones. The woman "was given to habits of intoxication" and, at the time the body was discovered, a candle was still burning on the table. Stevenson concluded the death was "nothing more than a casualty by fire." (Stevenson 1883)

(17) Circa 1866: An Englishman, about 30, who died of typhoid and whose corpse was found burning in its vault some *thirteen months after burial.* The day before the fire, "a foul smell was perceived in the church, and it was found to issue from a crevice in the floor immediately over the vault." The coffin and its outer shell had "burst opposite to the breast, and liquid matter was oozing from the body." The coffin was then filled with sawdust and the vault left open for the night. The next morning the vault was discovered burning "with a blueish flame and a most offensive smell." Said Stevenson: "Many persons set it down to spontaneous combustion, but it was found that one of the workmen had been smoking in the vault, and might have carelessly thrown down the lighted paper which he used." Stevenson suggested that this may have ignited the sawdust and the coffin's cloth cover, together with flammable gases from the putrefaction. (Stevenson 1883)

(18) Reported in 1870 in France: A drunken woman, her body discovered some two hours after she had gone to her bedroom. Her husband found the door extremely hot, and the room was entered by a window. The floor was still smoldering and there was considerable damage to the trunk of the body, with "a greasy black soot adhering to the vertebrae." The lower limbs were undamaged. While there was said to be "no fire in the grate," at least none remaining, the body was lying partially *across the hearth.* Its proximity to the fireplace is suggestive; Stevenson speculated, "The woman may have had matches about her, and in her intoxicated state an accident may have easily occurred. . . ." (Stevenson 1883)

(19) December 1885: Mrs. Patrick Rooney, at her Illinois home. Late one evening (sources give differing dates), she and her husband had continued to drink from a jug of spirits while their hired hand, John Larson, went upstairs to bed. Early the next morning, sick and vomiting, Larson made his way to the kitchen, where he saw everything was covered with "a black, greasy soot." On investigation, he found Rooney dead from asphyxiation. (One account states that Rooney's body was near the kitchen table, another that it was in a first-floor bedroom.) Near the kitchen table Larson discovered a hole burned through the floor. In the hole were Mrs. Rooney's remains: a few bones and a mound of ashes. We do not know whether the nearby kitchen stove was lit at the time Mrs. Rooney caught fire, but it may have been (or she may have been attempting to light it). That Mrs. Rooney's own body fat fuelled the fire is indicated by the greasy soot; she was said to weigh 200 pounds. (Eckert 1964; Gaddis 1967)

(20) 1908: Wilhelmina Dewar of Whitley Bay, near Blyth, England, who lived with her sister Margaret, both being retired schoolteachers. One evening Margaret urgently sought a neighbor, claiming that on arriving home she had discovered her sister's burned body. The body was lying on a bed which, however, was not scorched; neither was there evidence of fire damage elsewhere in the house. Under repeated questioning at an inquest, Margaret confessed "she had found her sister burned, but still alive, in a lower part of the house, and had helped her walk to the bed where she had died." How Wilhelmina had caught fire, and whether Margaret was in some way responsible, remained unanswered questions. Nevertheless, the evidence was sufficient to remove the case from the category of paranormal phenomena. (Gaddis 1967)

(21) December 1916: Miss Lillian C. Green, housekeeper for the proprietor of a hotel seven miles from Dover, New Jersey. She was found badly burned on the hotel's lower floor and later died at a Dover hospital. Gaddis (citing accounts in the *New York Herald*) stated: "The floor under her body was slightly scorched, but with the exception of her clothing, nothing else in the room showed the slightest trace of burns or possible origin of fire." Actually, the *Herald* reported that there "were no ashes from the clothing," leading investigators to suggest that Miss Green had been burned elsewhere. Subsequently "unmistakable evidence in traces of fire" was found on the *second floor,* revealing that her clothing had caught fire there. A county detective thought she might have set her clothes on fire with a cigarette, since the proprietor "told him that she frequently smoked cigarettes in her room." (Fort 1932; Gaddis 1967; *New York Herald* 1916)

(22) January 1930: Mrs. Nora Lake, 42, at her home in Kerhonkson, New York. Charles Fort cites the *New York Sun,* January 24, as reporting on a "coroner's inquest." Fort adds this quotation: "Although her body was severely burned, her clothing was not even scorched." A staff member of the New

New York Historical Society was unable to find the article in the *Sun;* however, a news item was found in the *New York World* of January 24. Mrs. Lake's body was found only two days earlier, so it is unlikely there was an inquest on the 24th. Firemen had been called to put out a fire in the kitchen and dining room. Although it is true Mrs. Lake's body was found burned yet fully clothed, it had also been "carefully arranged on the bed" upstairs, and her purse was "found open and rifled," missing cash she was known to have had. Police were understandably puzzled by the actions of the apparent criminal, but the evidence does not support a paranormal interpretation. (Fort 1932: *New York World* 1930)

(23) December 1949: Mrs. Ellen K. Coutres, 53, of Manchester, New Hampshire. She was found "dead from burns" as if she had been "a human torch." (The account does not indicate any extensive destruction of the body, merely that which might be attributable to clothing having caught fire.) That "flames had not ignited the wooden structure" need not present a mystery: Assuming the burning woman to have collapsed in the center of the room and away from combustibles, and depending on the amount of clothing on the body, it is plausible that the fire was just sufficient to cause the minimal destruction without (since flames burn upward) setting the floor on fire. Although it is reported that "the fire in her stove had been out for some time," it is entirely possible that it was *not* out at the time her clothing caught fire, and that it was actually the cause of the burning. (Gaddis 1967)

(24) July 1951: Mrs. Mary Reeser, 67, in St. Petersburg, Florida. Fireman called to her efficiency apartment extinguished a burning beam over a nearby partition. A big overstuffed chair had been reduced to its coiled springs and ashes; all that remained of the woman were a supposed skull, a large bone thought to be a hipbone, a charred liver attached to a piece of backbone, and a foot still in its slipper. An adjacent end table, plus the shade and wooden covering on a metal floor lamp had also been destroyed and a four-foot hole had been burned through the carpet. The floor was of concrete, which obviously prevented the fire from spreading. Heavy soot covered the ceiling and walls above a nearly level line about three and a half from the floor. Objects above the line had sufered heat damage. Under the remains was found a quantity of grease, leading investigators to conclude that the "plump" woman's own fat had fueled the fire. Mrs. Reeser had last been seen wearing a flammable nightdress and housecoat and smoking a cigarette, after having taken sleeping pills. (Allen 1951)

(25) May 1953: Mrs. Esther Dulin of Los Angeles, 30 years old. She "apparently fell asleep" in an overstuffed chair, and both chair and body had been "virtually consumed." In fact, the remains had burned completely through the floor and had dropped into the room below. According to an account of the case, "No other rooms or objects in the house were damaged." The

account is typical of those that emphasize mystery without providing crucial detail. For example, there is no mention of whether or not Mrs. Dulin smoked cigarettes. If we adopt this as a hypothesis, we have a plausible explanation of the case which invites comparison with the death of Mrs. Mary Reeser. (Gaddis 1967)

(26) May 1957: The mother of fireman Samuel Martin of West Philadelphia, Pennsylvania. The widow's charred body, lying face down, was discovered in the basement of their two-story house. Reportedly, "only the torso, burned beyond recognition, remained." The legs were said to have been "totally consumed," although the shoes (and presumably the feet) remained. Over an area of about four feet square around the body was a stain, "not oil, as it first appered to be, but residue from the consumed body." Mrs. Martin's remains were found in front of a coal furnace in which there was supposedly no fire and the metal cold. The close proximity of the body to the furnace is noteworthy, however. Possibly the fire had gone out (and the metal subsequently cooled) before the body was discovered. As another possibility, Mrs. Martin's clothes may have caught fire as she *attempted* to light the furnace. (Gaddis 1967)

(27) January 1959: Jack Larber, a 72-year-old patient at the Laguna Honda Home in San Francisco. On the last day of the month, Larber had been fed his meal by an attendant, who returned a few minutes later to find Larber's clothing aflame. The fire was put out with blankets, but Larber died on February 2 of third-degree burns. Gaddis notes that Larber was a nonsmoker, but neglects to mention that he was lying in bed or that he was in a psychiatric ward for senile patients. According to the *San Francisco Examiner,* "Because of their mental state, none of the five fellow inmates of the ward could relate what happened." A police inspector "said it appeared one of the inmates may have unwittingly tipped a burning match which ignited Larber's clothes." (Gaddis 1967; *San Francisco Examiner* 1959)

(28) November 1960: Five men who perished by fire in an automobile along a rural road in Pike County, Kentucky. Their bodies were "charred beyond recognition." The right front door was open and blood was found nearby. Foul play was ruled out after autopsies revealed a significant amount of carbon monoxide in the bodies, proving that the men had been breathing when the fire occurred. Apparently no tests were made for traces of flammable liquids such as gasoline. A coroner's jury ruled the deaths accidental, although the cause of the fire was not determined. Since the car had "gone over a slight embankment" and "was badly damaged by fire, "there would seem to be the possibility that the gas tank ruptured and caught fire, resulting in the men's deaths. (Michell and Rickard 1977; *Pike County News* 1960)

(29) December 1966: Dr. J. Irving Bentley, a 92-year-old physician of Coudersport, Pennsylvania. Friends visited him at about 9:00 P.M. on the 4th. The next morning a meter reader noticed a "light-blue smoke of unusual odor"

likened to that from burning oil. Upstairs, a hole about 2½ by 4 feet had burned through the bathroom floor. At the edge was a leg burned off at the knee; atop a basement post was a knee joint; and on the basement floor was a heap of ashes. Contrary to some claims, his skull was also found. "Many times before" the doctor had dropped hot ashes from his pipe upon his clothes, which "were dotted with burn spots from previous incidents." In this instance, burns reportedly found on the bedroom rug indicated he had set his clothes afire and had made his way, with the aid of his walker, to the bathroom, where he had vainly attempted to extinguish the flames. He had managed to shed his robe, found smoldering in the bathtub, and broken remains of what was apparently a water pitcher were found in the toilet. (Arnold 1976)

(30) August 1982: An unidentified Chicago woman who (according to a City News Bureau bulletin) had been walking down a street on the morning of August 5 and "burst into flames for no apparent reason, police said." An eyewitness allegedly "saw her burning and then she fell." Later the CNB added to its bulletin a suggestion of spontaneous human combustion. Still later, however, an autopsy revealed that the victim had been dead *before* the burning took place, and the Chicago crime lab found traces of hydrocarbon accelerants on her clothing. The case obviously did not involve spontaneous combustion, but warranted a homicide investigation. (*Orlando Sentinel* 1982)

The thirty cases we have presented include a wide variety of circumstances that precludes a single, simplistic explanation for all unusual burning deaths, just as one cannot explain all "flying saucer" reports by attributing them to weather balloons. Obviously, cases must be judged on an individual basis. We can, however, make some general observations.

The cases include those in which the victims were not given to intoxication as well as those in which they were. In the latter instances, alcohol may have indeed been a contributing factor, although not in the way some nineteenth-century theorists imagined. A drunken person would be more likely to be careless with fire and less able to properly respond to an accident.

Homicide was confessed to in two instances (10, 13) and was reportedly proved in another (14). It was suspected in a limited number of additional instances, although possibly erroneously, since there are alternate plausible explanations for these cases.

It is true that in some of the cases an immediate source for the ignition does not obviously present itself, but insufficient data seems the problem here. For example, in case 25 we simply do not know whether the victim (who "apparently fell asleep" in an overstuffed chair) was a smoker or nonsmoker. Several accounts emphasized that there was "no fire" in the grate or stove near which a particular victim was found. But we find the proximity of the fireplaces in these instances highly suggestive, and we hypothesize that the victims may have been *attempting* to light the fire, or that the fire went out *before* the victim was discovered. In most cases, however, a probable cause could be assigned to the conflagration and in none was a potential naturalistic explanation ruled out.

In some of the fires, damage to surroundings was relatively minimal, yet we found plausible explanations for this, as for example the floor being of concrete (24) or the fire being interrupted in its progress when it was discovered and extinguished (6).

Proponents of SHC/PC frequently emphasize those rare cases in which the clothing or bedclothing (if the victim was abed) was reportedly undamaged, but we wonder what point advocates are attempting to make. (Surely they are not suggesting that the victims had fireproof clothes; if they intend to imply that the fire itself is of a mysterious, selective nature, then they must concede that those cases in which the clothing *has* burned—the overwhelming majority of cases—are *not* instances of SHC or PC.) In the three instances of this type that we studied (15, 20, 21), no indication of anything paranormal was evident.

Interestingly, melted human fat seems to have augmented the burning in numerous cases, with reports of "greasy soot and ashes" being quite common. In examples 19 and 24, the victims are known to have been excessively fat, and this may be true of other cases as well. Most accounts simply failed to state whether the victim was fat or lean. In the single instance (9) in which it was reported that the victim was "not fat," there was considerable supplementary fuel provided by the bedding upon which he had burned. Frequently, there was considerable such combustible material under the victim, and this had burned and obviously aided in the destruction of the body. In addition to bedding, there were overstuffed chairs and even wooden flooring.

In summary, in two years of investigating reported cases of spontaneous human combustion and/or preternatural combustibility, we found no credible evidence to warrant postulating such phenomena. On the contrary—except in cases in which crucial data was woefully lacking—we found that plausible, naturalistic explanations could easily be provided. We conclude that proponents who argue merely from effect, ignoring the important question of cause, are destined to remain forever mystified. We would suggest that they temper their understandable thirst for mystery by doing more careful research: In three of the twentieth-century cases (21, 22, 27) we were readily able to uncover additional data which rendered the cases far less mysterious than they had been represented by SHC/PC advocates.

Select Bibliography

Adelson, Lester. 1952. *Journal of Criminal Law, Criminology and Police Science* (March-April).

Allen, W. S. 1951. "Weird Cremation." *True Detective,* December, 42-45, 93-94.

Annual Register. 1763. 6:95.

Arnold, Larry E. 1976. "The Flaming Fate of Dr. John Irving Bentley." *Pursuit,* Fall, 75-79.

Beck, Theodric R., and John B. Beck. 1835. *Elements of Medical Jurisprudence,* 60-68. 5th ed. Vol. 2. Albany, N.Y.: O. Steele et al.

Eckert, Allan W. 1964. "The Baffling Burning Death." *True,* May, 33, 104-112.

Fort, Charles. [1932] 1974. *Wild Talents.* Reprint in *The Books of Charles Fort.* Ann Arbor, Mich.: University Microfilms.

Gaddis, Vincent H. 1967. *Mysterious Fires and Lights.* New York: David McKay.

Gentlemen's Magazine. 1746. 16:368.

Lewes, George Henry. 1861. "Spontaneous Combustion." *Blackwood's Edinburgh Magazine* 89 (April): 385-402.

Michell, John, and Robert J. M. Rickard. 1977. *Phenomena: A Book of Wonders,* 34-35. New York: Pantheon.

New York Herald. 1916. 27-28 December.

New York World. 1930. 24 January.

Orlando Sentinel. 1982. 6, 10 August.

Pike County News (Kentucky). 1960. 23 November; 1, 15 December.

Stevenson, Thomas. 1883. *The Principles and Practice of Medical Jurisprudence,* 718-727. 3rd ed. Philadelphia: Lea.

NOTES

Chapter 1. Introduction

1. For the discussion of "supernatural" vs. "paranormal," as well as subsequent paragraphs treating such topics as skepticism, debunking, etc., I am indebted to Paul Kurtz, "Debunking, Neutrality, and Skepticism in Science," in *Science Confronts the Paranormal,* ed. Kendrick Frazier (Buffalo: Prometheus Books, 1986), 5–12; Marcello Truzzi, "Zetetic Ruminations on Skepticism and Anomalies in Science," *Zetetic Scholar,* nos. 12–13 (1987): 7–20; and Jerome Clark, "Confessions of a Fortean Skeptic," *Zetetic Scholar,* no. 11 (1983): 7–14.

2. The NORC survey was reported in the January-February *American Health* and subsequently discussed in *Skeptical Inquirer* 11, no. 4 (Summer 1987): 333–334, and in Robert C. Cowen, "Research Notebook" column, *Christian Science Monitor,* 7 July 1987.

3. Quoted in *Skeptical Inquirer* 11, no. 4 (Summer 1987): 334.

4. Owen S. Rachleff, *The Occult Conceit* (Chicago: Cowles, 1971), ix.

5. Paul Tabori, *The Natural Science of Stupidity* (Philadelphia: Chilton, 1959), 154.

6. W. I. B. Beveridge, *The Art of Scientific Investigation* (New York: Vintage, n.d.), 115-116; Elie A. Shneour, "Occam's Razor," *Skeptical Inquirer* 10 (1986): 310-313.

7. Sir Arthur Conan Doyle, "The Adventure of the Bruce-Partington Plans." This, together with the quotations at the beginning of each chapter, is from *The Complete Sherlock Holmes* (Garden City, N.Y.: Garden City Books, n.d.).

Chapter 2. Haunted Stairs

1. An earlier article on the alleged haunting is Joe Nickell, "The Ghost at Mackenzie House," *Canada West,* Fall 1979, 16–18. Other, less skeptical accounts are in Sheila Hervey, *Some Canadian Ghosts* (Richmond Hill, Ontario: Simon & Schuster of Canada, 1973), 106–114, and Susy Smith, "Turbulence in Toronto," chap. 2 in *Ghosts Around the House* (New York: World Publishing, 1970), 38–50.

2. Mrs. Edmunds's statement to the *Toronto Telegram* is given in Smith, "Turbulence in Toronto," 44.

3. Robert A. Baker, Professor of Psychology, lecture on "ghostbusting," University of Kentucky, 30 October 1987.

4. Quoted in Smith, "Turbulence in Toronto," 46.

5. Ibid.

6. Rom Harré and Roger Lamb, "Contagion," in *The Encyclopedic Dictionary of Psychology* (Cambridge, Mass.: MIT Press, 1983), 119.

7. Hans van Kampen, "The Case of the Lost Panda," *Skeptical Inquirer* 4, no. 1 (Fall 1979): 48–50.

8. Hervey, *Some Canadian Ghosts,* 110–114.

9. Ibid.

10. Smith, "Turbulence in Toronto," 38.

11. Felix Glied, personal communication, cited in Nickell, "The Ghost at Mackenzie House," 17.

12. Editorial, *Toronto Daily Star,* 28 June 1960; portions cited in Hervy, *Some Canadian Ghosts,* 110–111.

13. Smith, "Turbulence in Toronto," 43–47; Hervey, *Some Canadian Ghosts,* 107–109. See also Richard Winer and Nancy Osborn, *Haunted Houses* (New York: Bantam, 1979), 133–135.

14. Mackenzie Homestead tour guide, personal communication, 21 August 1972.

15. Tony Vrewey, personal communication, 8 May 1973.

16. Ibid.

Chapter 3. Gem of Death

1. Simon Welfare and John Fairley, *Arthur C. Clarke's Mysterious World* (New York: A & W Publishers, 1980), 51.

2. Richard M. Garvin, *The Crystal Skull* (Garden City, N.Y.: Doubleday, 1973), 6.

3. John Sinclair, "Crystal Skull of Doom," *Fate,* March 1962, 64–68.

4. Garvin, *Crystal Skull,* 6.

5. Welfare and Fairley, *Mysterious World,* 51.

6. F. A. Mitchell-Hedges, *Land of Wonder and Fear* (New York: Century Company, 1931), 94.

7. F. A. Mitchell-Hedges, *Danger My Ally* (London: Elek Books, 1954), 243.

8. Sibley S. Morrill, *Ambrose Bierce, F. A. Mitchell-Hedges and the Crystal Skull* (San Francisco: Caledon Press, 1972), 66–67.

9. G. M. Morant, "A Morphological Comparison of Two Crystal Skulls," *Man* 36 (July 1936): 105.

10. Ibid., 105–107.

11. Adrian Digby, "Comments on the Morphological Comparison of Two Crystal Skulls," *Man* 36 (July 1936): 107–109.

12. Frank Dorland, quoted in Garvin, *Crystal Skull*, 84; letter to Joe Nickell, 20 May 1983.

13. Norman Hammond, letter to Joe Nickell, 27 May 1983.

14. George Frederick Kunz, *Gems and Precious Stones* (New York: Scientific Publishing, 1890), 285–286.

15. Welfare and Fairley, *Mysterious World*, 55.

16. D. R. Barrett, letter to Joe Nickell (with enclosure: copy of museum registration notes), 29 July 1982.

17. Kunz, *Gems and Precious Stones*, 285.

18. John Sampson White, Associate Curator-in-Charge, Division of Mineralogy, Smithsonian Institution, letter to Joe Nickell, 30 November 1982.

19. Gordon F. Ekholm, letters to Joe Nickell, 5 January; 1 February 1983.

20. Folke Henschen, *The Human Skull: A Cultural History* (New York: Praeger, 1966), 135–146.

21. Ibid., 135.

22. George Kennedy, quoted in Garvin, *Crystal Skull*, 82.

23. Garvin, *Crystal Skull*, 29.

24. Norman Hammond, *Lubaantun: A Classic Maya Realm* (Cambridge, Mass.: Peabody Museum of Archaeology and Ethnology, Harvard University, 1975).

25. Norman Hammond, letter to Joe Nickell, 27 May 1983.

26. Ibid.

27. F. A. Mitchell-Hedges, *Danger My Ally*, 203.

28. Anna Mitchell-Hedges in Garvin, *Crystal Skull*, photo no. 25 following p. 38.

29. Garvin, *Crystal Skull*, 13–14.

30. Welfare and Fairley, *Mysterious World*, 52.

31. Mitchell-Hedges, *Danger My Ally*, 189.

32. Sinclair, "Crystal Skull of Doom," 65.

33. Morrill, *Bierce, Mitchell-Hedges, Skull*, 26–27.

34. Anna Mitchell-Hedges, letter to Joe Nickell, 1 March 1983.

35. Anna Mitchell-Hedges, letter to Joe Nickell, 25 April 1983.

36. Ibid.

37. F. A. Mitchell-Hedges, *Danger My Ally*; see also obituary, *New York Times,* 13 June 1959.

38. Morrill, *Bierce, Mitchell-Hedges, Skull,* 55.

39. F. A. Mitchell-Hedges, *Battles with Giant Fish* (Boston: Small, Maynard, 1924), photos facing pp. 196, 230.

40. Mitchell-Hedges, *Danger My Ally,* 191.

41. Morrill, *Bierce, Mitchell-Hedges, Skull,* 28; Welfare and Fairley, *Mysterious World,* 53.

42. Ibid.

43. Anna Mitchell-Hedges, letters to Joe Nickell, 1 March; 25 April 1983.

44. Morrill, *Bierce, Mitchell-Hedges, Skull,* 28.

45. Digby, "Comments on the Morphological Comparison," 108; Morant, "Morphological Comparison," 105.

46. See Morant, "Morphological Comparison," illus. b facing p. 105.

47. Mitchell-Hedges, *Danger My Ally,* 240.

48. Anna Mitchell-Hedges, letter to Joe Nickell, 25 April 1983.

49. Sydney Burney, letter to George Vaillant, American Museum of Natural History, 21 March 1933.

50. Norman Hammond, letter to Joe Nickell, 27 May 1983.

51. H. J. Braunholtz, "Two Crystal Skulls. Further Comments . . .," *Man* 36 (July 1936): 109.

52. Anna Mitchell-Hedges, letter to Joe Nickell, 25 April 1983.

53. Frank Dorland, letter to Joe Nickell, 20 May 1983.

54. Kunz, *Gems and Precious Stones,* 286–287.

55. Joe Rothstein, letter to Joe Nickell, 21 January 1983.

56. F. A. Mitchell-Hedges, "Atlantis Was No Myth but the Cradle of American Races . . .," *New York American,* 10 March 1935.

57. Mitchell-Hedges, *Danger My Ally,* 243; caption to illus. facing p. 241.

58. Sinclair, "Crystal Skull of Doom," 67.

59. Garvin, *Crystal Skull,* 91.

60. Anna Mitchell-Hedges, letter to Joe Nickell, 25 April 1983.

61. Sinclair, "Crystal Skull of Doom," 67.

62. Garvin, *Crystal Skull,* 90–91, 100.

63. Sinclair, "Crystal Skull of Doom," 66.

64. Frank Dorland, letter to Joe Nickell, 20 May 1983.

65. Frank Dorland, in Garvin, *Crystal Skull,* 99–100.

66. Garvin, *Crystal Skull,* 100; photo facing p. 39.

67. George Frederick Kunz, *The Curious Lore of Precious Stones* (1913; reprint, New York: Dover, 1971).

68. Anna Mitchell-Hedges, letter to Joe Nickell, 1 March 1983.

Chapter 4. Phantom Pictures

1. John Mulholland, *Beware Familiar Spirits* (1938; reprint, New York: Scribner, 1979), 27–45. Milbourne Christopher, *ESP, Seers and Psychics: What the Occult Really Is* (New York: Corwell, 1970), 175.
2. Christopher, *ESP,* 175.
3. Mulholland, *Beware Familiar Spirits,* 49–70.
4. Christopher, *ESP,* 175–176.
5. Ibid., 174–187.
6. Mulholland, *Beware Familiar Spirits,* 147–148.
7. James Randi, "A Skotography Scam Exposed," *Skeptical Inquirer* 7, no. 1 (Fall 1982): 59–61.
8. Christopher, *ESP,* 174–175.
9. M. Lamar Keene (as told to Allen Spraggett), *The Psychic Mafia* (New York: St. Martin, 1976).
10. Ibid., 41.
11. Ibid., 95–114.
12. The names of our informants and other details are in our confidential report, "An Investigation of Some Alleged 'Spirit' Pictures," 1 August 1985. This report and various affidavits and statements are now part of police files in the city where the deception was performed.
13. Robert H. van Outer, personal communication, 30 May 1985.
14. Mark Comley, personal communication, 7 June 1985.
15. Further details are in our report (see n. 12).
16. Keene, *Psychic Mafia,* 110–111.
17. Ibid., 111.
18. Ibid., 54.

Chapter 5. Vanished!

1. Frank Edwards, *Strangest of All* (New York: Signet, 1962), 102.
2. Ibid., 103.
3. Joe Nickell, "The Oliver Lerch Disappearance: A Postmortem," *Fate,* March 1980, 61–65.
4. Joseph Rosenberger, "What Happened to Oliver Lerch?" *Fate,* September 1950, 28–31.
5. Nickell, "Postmortem," 61ff.
6. Nickell, "Postmortem," 62–63. *South Bend Tribune* clippings, 14 May 1967; 9 December 1974; 21 August 1979.
7. John Michell and J. M. Rickard, *Phenomena: A Book of Wonders* (New York: Pantheon, 1977), 98.
8. Eddie Collard, letter to Joe Nickell, 11 September 1979.

9. Name withheld on request, letter to Joe Nickell, 20 July 1979.

10. Ambrose Bierce,"Charles Ashmore's Trail," in *Can Such Things Be?* (1893; reprint, New York: Albert & Charles Boni, 1924), 421–424.

11. Name withheld on request, letter to Joe Nickell, 30 August 1979.

12. Nickell, "Postmortem," 64.

13. Harold T. Wilkins, *Mysterious Disappearances of Men and Women in the U.S.A., Britain and Europe* (Girard, Kans.: Haldeman-Julius Publications, 1948), 4–5.

14. Robert Schadewald, "Fortean Fakes and Folklore," *Pursuit* 11, no. 3 (Summer 1978): 98–100.

15. Robert Schadewald, "David Lang Vanishes . . . FOREVER," *Fate,* December 1977, 54.

16. David Wallechinsky and Irving Wallace, *The People's Almanac* (Garden City, N.Y.: Doubleday, 1975), 1370–1371.

17. Schadewald, "David Lang Vanishes . . . FOREVER," 55–56.

18. Ibid., 54–60.

19. Ibid., 59.

20. Jay Robert Nash, *Among the Missing* (New York: Simon & Schuster, 1978), 330.

21. Ibid., 330.

22. Eleanor R. Falkenberry, letter to author, 4 December 1979; Milo B. Howard, Jr., letters to author, 8, 20 November 1979; Office of Dallas County (Alabama) County Clerk, undated, unsigned note affixed to Joe Nickell's letter of 30 October 1979.

23. Isaac Asimov, *Asimov's Guide to the Bible,* vol. 1 (New York: Equinox Books, 1971), 480.

24. Gertrude Jobes, *Dictionary of Mythology, Folklore and Symbols,* vol. 2 (New York: Scarecrow, 1961), 1215.

25. Wallechinski, *People's Almanac,* 1371.

26. "Fairy," *Encyclopaedia Britannica,* 1973.

27. Ibid.

28. Schadewald, "David Lang Vanishes . . . FOREVER," 60; Schadewald, "Fortean Fakes and Folklore," 98.

29. Wilkins, *Mysterious Disappearances,* 5.

30. Schadewald, "David Lang Vanishes . . . FOREVER," 60.

31. Ibid., 55; see also Jack Burnett, "Mystery: The Story of David Lang," *Cumberland Magazine,* Winter 1977-78, 31, 47.

32. Curtis D. MacDougall, *Hoaxes* (New York: Dover, 1958), 5.

33. Walter Neale, *Life of Ambrose Bierce* (1929; reprint, New York: AMS, 1969), 372.

34. Ibid., 59.

35. Martin Gardner, *Fads and Fallacies in the Name of Science* (New York:

Dover, 1957), 42–54.

36. Elliott O'Donnell, *Strange Disappearances* (New York: University Books, 1972), 52–92.

37. Robert Dale Owen, *Footfalls on the Boundary of Another World* (Philadelphia: Lippincott, 1869), 319–320.

38. E. F. Bleiler, ed., *Ghost and Horror Stories of Ambrose Bierce* (New York: Dover, 1964), xviii.

39. Cora L. Daniels and Prof. C. M. Stevens, eds., *Encyclopaedia of Superstitions, Folklore and the Occult Sciences* (1903; reprint, Detroit: Gale Research, 1971), 1255.

40. Neale, *Ambrose Bierce,* 429ff.

41. Paul Fatout, *Ambrose Bierce: The Devil's Lexicographer* (Norman, Okla.: Oklahoma University Press, 1951), 308.

42. For an expanded discussion of Bierce's disappearance, see Joe Nickell, "Literary Investigation," Ph.D. diss., University of Kentucky, 1987.

Chapter 6. Double Trouble

1. Elinor J. Brecher, "Two of a Kind: Babies Born in Louisville Almost Had Twin Mothers," *Louisville Courier-Journal* (Kentucky), 9 February 1981.

2. C. G. Jung, "Synchronicity: An Acausal Connecting Principle," in *The Collected Works of C. G. Jung,* ed. Sir Herbert Read et al., Bollingen Series, no. 20 (New York: Pantheon, 1960), 418–519.

3. Jung, "Synchronicity," 424.

4. Gustav Jahoda, *The Psychology of Superstition* (Baltimore: Penguin, 1970), 118.

5. C. E. M. Hansel, *ESP: A Scientific Evaluation* (New York: Scribner, 1966), 194.

6. Luis W. Alvarez, "A Pseudo Experience in Parapsychology," letter in *Science* 148 (1965): 1541.

7. Ruma Falk, "On Coincidences," *Skeptical Inquirer* 6, no. 2 (Winter 1981-81): 24–25.

8. Alan Vaughan, "The Riddle of Coincidence," *Fate,* January 1980, 66.

9. Wyatt Blassingame, *Science Catches the Criminal* (New York: Dodd, Mead, 1975), 12.

10. T. Dickerson Cooke, *The Blue Book of Crime: Science of Crime Detection* (Chicago: Institute of Applied Science, 1959), 43.

11. C. A. Mitchell, *The Expert Witness* (New York: D. Appleton, 1923), 26–27.

12. For photos of Beck and Thomas, see Jurgen Thorwald, *The Century of the Detective* (New York: Harcourt, Brace & World, 1964), illustration facing p. 84.

13. Douglas G. Browne and Alan Brock, *Fingerprints: Fifty Years of Scientific Crime Detection* (New York: Dutton, 1954), 126.

14. Thorwald, *Detective,* 95.

15. Homer A. Boynton, Jr., letter to Joe Nickell, 16 February 1979. As with most of the following material, this was cited in Joe Nickell, "The Two 'Will Wests': A New Verdict," *Journal of Police Science and Administration* 8, no. 4 (1980): 406–413.

16. Jean Milner, letters to author, 20 March; 9 May 1979.

17. Robert D. Olsen, Sr., "The 'Will West' Case," *Identification News,* November 1983, 3–15. (Mr. Olsen and I both lectured on the West case at the 68th Annual Conference of the International Association of Identification in Orlando, Florida, 16 August 1983.)

18. A. V. Iannarelli, letter to Joe Nickell, 17 April 1979.

19. Ibid.

20. P. J. Dunleavy, letter to Joe Nickell, 29 May 1979.

21. Steven G. Vandenberg, letter to Joe Nickell, 26 June 1979.

22. James M. Puckett, letter to Joe Nickell, 7 June 1979.

23. "Double Trouble," *Louisville Courier-Journal* (Kentucky), 5 October 1984.

24. Eugene Block, *Fingerprinting: Magic Weapon Against Crime* (New York: David McKay, 1969), 17.

25. Ibid., 25.

26. Don Whitehead, *The FBI Story* (New York: Random House, 1956), 133. According to Whitehead, although New York State adopted fingerprinting for Sing Sing in 1903, it was not installed at Leavenworth until the following year (the same year that St. Louis became "the first American city to switch from the Bertillon system to fingerprints").

27. Thorwald, *Detective,* 95.

Chapter 7. Psychic Prospectors

1. Leslie Shepard, ed., *Encyclopedia of Occultism and Parapsychology,* 2nd ed., vol. 1 (Detroit: Gale Research, 1984), 362.

2. Richard Cavendish, ed., *Encyclopedia of the Unexplained: Magic, Occultism and Parapsychology* (London: Routledge & Kegan Paul, 1974), 75.

3. Ibid., 13–14.

4. Evon Z. Vogt and Ray Hyman, *Water Witching U.S.A.,* 2nd ed. (Chicago: University of Chicago Press, 1979), 13.

5. Ibid., 13–14.

6. Charles Mackay, *Memoirs of Extraordinary Popular Delusions and the Madness of Crowds* (1852; reprint, Toronto: Coles Publishing, 1980), 291–294.

7. Quoted in Vogt and Hyman, *Water Witching,* 14–15.

8. Vogt and Hyman, *Water Witching, passim;* Christopher Bird, *The Divining Hand* (New York: Dutton, 1979), *passim.*

9. Vogt and Hyman, *Water Witching,* fig. 10 following p. 52.

10. Bird, *Divining Hand,* 55.

11. Ibid., 209.

12. Ibid., 55.

13. Vogt and Hyman, *Water Witching, passim;* Bird, *Divining Hand, passim.*

14. Bird, *Divining Hand,* 227–228.

15. Venture Bookshop advertisement, *Fate,* April 1985, 18.

16. Martin Gardner, *Fads and Fallacies in the Name of Science* (New York: Dover, 1957), 109.

17. Quoted in Milbourne Christopher, *ESP, Seers and Psychics: What the Occult Really Is* (New York: Crowell, 1970), 125.

18. Christopher, *ESP,* 131.

19. Ibid., 122.

20. Bird, *Divining Hand,* 5.

21. Ibid., 4–6.

22. Gardner, *Fads and Fallacies,* 112.

23. Christopher, *ESP,* 139.

24. L. A. Dale et al., "Dowsing: A Field Experiment in Water Divining," *Journal of American Society for Psychical Research* 45 (1951): 3–16; cited in Vogt and Hyman, *Water Witching,* 72–73.

25. Christopher, *ESP,* 140–141.

26. James Randi, "A Controlled Test of Dowsing Abilities," *Skeptical Inquirer* 4, no. 1 (Fall 1979): 16–20.

27. See Jim Christy, *Rough Road to the North* (New York: Doubleday, 1980), 144; *Contemporary Authors,* vol. 110 (Detroit: Gale Research, 1984), 376; Joe Nickell, "Gold Rush: Signs of the Times," *Canada West* 11, no. 1 (Spring 1981): 2–8.

28. Rossel Hope Robbins, *The Encyclopedia of Witchcraft and Demonology* (New York: Crown, 1959), 137–138.

29. John Locke, 1591; quoted in *Oxford English Dictionary,* vol. 3 (1933; reprint, Oxford: Clarendon Press, 1933), 629: "Dowse."

30. See Murray Morgan, *One Man's Gold Rush,* with photographs by E. A. Hegg (Seattle: University of Washington Press, 1972), photo on p. 156; Joe Nickell, "Gold Rush: Signs of the Times," 2–8.

31. As far as I know, this photo—seen while I was searching the Yukon Archives' photos for the Dawson City Museum—has gone unpublished.

32. The following account is adapted from the original newspaper article: Joe Nickell, "Not Recommended for Serious Mineral Exploration," *Yukon News,* 1 September 1976.

33. Here are the individual guesses: TEST SERIES NO. 1 (A-J): Stevenson, tobacco A, gold G; Leverman, tobacco A, gold B, E, J; Fritz (declined tobacco test), gold H; Wilks, tobacco E, J, gold H. TEST SERIES NO. 2 (1-10): Stevenson, tobacco 4, gold 10; Leverman, tobacco, 1, 5, 9, 10, gold 8; Fritz (declined tobacco test), gold 2; Wilks, tobacco 2, 4, 5, 9, gold 7, 10.

34. The contents of the boxes were as follows: TEST SERIES NO. 1: A, cigarette; D, gold ring; J, pyrite ("fool's gold"). TEST SERIES NO. 2: 8, gold nugget; all other boxes in the two series either were empty or contained nuts, bolts, etc.

Chapter 8. Celestial Painting

1. Jody Brant Smith, *The Image of Guadalupe* (Garden City, N.Y.: Doubleday, 1983), 4.

2. Donald Demarest and Coley Taylor, eds., *The Dark Virgin* (N.p.: Academy Guild Press, 1956), 2.

3. G. Gordon Henderson, introduction to *The Apparitions of Guadalupe as Historical Events*, by Luis Medina Ascensio (Washington, D.C.: Center for Applied Research in the Apostolate, 1979), iv.

4. G. Gordon Henderson, introduction to *A Major Guadalupan Question Resolved*, by Ernest J. Burrus (Washington, D.C.: Center for Applied Research in the Apostolate, 1979), v.

5. Cleofas Callero, trans., *Nican Mopohua*, in Smith, *Image of Guadalupe*, 121-135.

6. Ascensio, *Apparitions of Guadalupe*, 1.

7. Jacques LaFaye, *Quetzalcoatl and Guadalupe: The Formation of Mexican National Consciousness 1531-1813* (Chicago: University of Chicago Press, 1976), 231-253.

8. Burrus, *Major Guadalupan Question*, 3.

9. Smith, *Image of Guadalupe*, 21.

10. Ernest J. Burrus, *Major Guadalupan Question*, vi; id., *The Oldest Copy of the Nican Mopohua* (Washington, D.C.: Center for Applied Research in the Apostolate, 1981), 4.

11. Smith, *Image of Guadalupe*, 121.

12. Ibid., 18-19.

13. Joe Nickell, *Inquest on the Shroud of Turin*, upd. ed. (Buffalo: Prometheus Books, 1987), 43ff, 119ff.

14. Anna Brownell Jameson, *Legends of the Madonna as Represented in the Fine Arts* (London: Longmans, Green, 1902), xxxiv.

15. Smith, *Image of Guadalupe*, 61.

16. Marcello Craveri, *The Life of Jesus*, trans. Charles Lam Markmann (New York: Grove, 1967), 27-28.

17. Ibid.

18. Smith, *Image of Guadalupe,* 20.

19. "Virgen de Guadalupe," *Enciclopedia de Mexico* (Ciudad de Mexico, 1878), 4, 15.

20. Smith, *Image of Guadalupe,* 10–11.

21. "Mexico," *Encyclopaedia Britannica,* 1973.

22. Major Arthur De Bles, *How to Distinguish the Saints in Art* (New York: Art Culture Press, 1925), 35.

23. Philip Serna Callahan, *The Tilma under Infra-red Radiation* (Washington, D.C.: Center for Applied Research in the Apostolate, 1981), 20.

24. Smith, *Image of Guadalupe,* 68–69.

25. De Bles, *Saints in Art,* 35; George Ferguson, *Signs and Symbols in Christian Art* (New York: Oxford University Press, 1967), 89; F. R. Webber, *Church Symbolism* (Cleveland: J. H. Jansen, 1938), 161.

26. Webber, *Church Symbolism,* 181; De Bles, *Saints in Art,* 41.

27. Smith, *Image of Guadalupe,* 69.

28. Webber, *Church Symbolism,* 71; De Bles, *Saints in Art,* 27.

29. De Bles, *Saints in Art,* 40.

30. Callahan, *Infra-red Radiation,* 8.

31. Ibid., 12.

32. Ibid., 10.

33. Ibid., 18.

34. Ibid.

35. Smith, *Image of Guadalupe,* 12, 68–69.

36. Ibid., 70.

37. Callahan, *Infra-red Radiation,* 9ff.

38. Ibid., 8.

39. Ibid., 18, 20.

40. Ibid., 17.

41. Ibid., 9.

42. Ibid., 13.

43. Ibid., 15.

44. Ibid., 43.

45. Ibid., 16.

46. Ibid.

47. Smith, *Image of Guadalupe,* 29, 31.

48. Callahan, *Infra-red Radiation,* 18.

49. Mark M. Johnson, *Idea to Image* (Cleveland, Ohio: Cleveland Museum of Art, 1980), 65.

50. Callahan, *Infra-red Radiation,* 10, 36.

51. See H. W. Janson, *History of Art* (Englewood Cliffs, N.J.: Prentice-Hall, 1963), colorplates 26, 31, 45; De Bles, *Saints in Art,* 30; Estelle M. Hurll,

The Madonna in Art (Boston: L. C. Page, 1897), 112ff; Rudolph Reni-Pallavicini, *The Most Beautiful Women in the World* (Albuquerque, N.M.: American Classified College Press, 1975), 4–25; Jameson, *Legends of the Madonna,* 1i.

52. Jameson, *Legends of the Madonna,* 4–5; De Bles, *Saints in Art,* 35.

53. Heather Child and Dorothy Colles, *Christian Symbols Ancient and Modern* (New York: Scribner, 1971), 219.

54. Smith, *Image of Guadalupe,* 20–21.

55. Callahan, *Infra-red Radiation,* 30–44.

56. Glenn Taylor, personal communication, Lexington, Kentucky, 4 October 1983.

57. Patrick Tierney, "The Arts," *Omni,* September 1983, 174, 190.

58. Smith, *Image of Guadalupe,* 79–83, 111ff.

59. Cullen Murphy, "Shreds of Evidence," *Harper's,* November 1981, 44.

60. Terry Kay, "Jesus in Jasper," *Atlanta Weekly,* 11 September 1983, 18ff.

61. James C. Shearer, David C. Peters, Gerald Hoepfner, and Travers Newton, "FTIR in the Service of Art Conservation," *Analytical Chemistry* 55 (July 1983): 874A–880A.

62. Smith, *Image of Guadalupe,* 107.

Chapter 9. Bleeding Door

1. Robert E. Bell, *Dictionary of Classical Mythology* (Santa Barbara: ABC/CLIO, 1982), 29.

2. Ibid., 30.

3. D. Scott Rogo, *Miracles* (New York: Dial, 1982), 164–68.

4. "Virgin Mary 'Miracle' that Drew Thousands Is Exposed as a Hoax," *Louisville Courier-Journal* (Kentucky), 18 January 1986, p. A4.

5. Rogo, *Miracles,* 164–169; E. Cobham Brewer, *Dictionary of Miracles* (Philadelphia: Lippincott, 1984), 184. See also John Coulson, ed., *The Saints: A Concise Biographical Dictionary* (New York: Hawthorne Books, 1958), 238–239.

6. Stith Thompson's *Motif-Index of Folk Literature,* rev. ed., vol. 2 of 6 vols. (Bloomington: Indiana University Press, 1955), 446.

7. Perrott Phillips, ed., *Out of this World: The Illustrated Library of the Bizarre and Extraordinary,* vol. 12 of 24 vols. (N.p.: Phoebus/BPC, 1978), 58.

8. Ibid.

9. This is located in Morgan County, Kentucky. On maps the name is often given as "Deadling Branch": See *Kentucky County Maps* (Appleton, Wisc.: Privately printed by C. J. Puetz, n.d.), 95. For a brief sketch of the story that follows, see Joe Nickell, "Morgan County Cemeteries: A Brief History," introduction to *Morgan County Cemetery Records,* comp. J. Wendell Nickell, Ella T. Nickell, and Joe Nickell, vol. 1 (West Liberty, Ky.: Privately printed,

1978); entry for "Eversole Graveyard," vol. 3, also gives data on the cemetery that is described.

10. Federal census records for 1840-1870, Morgan County, Kentucky. (A single man with the name Eversole was listed on the 1860 census.

11. Federal census records for 1880, Morgan County, Kentucky, North Fork Voting Precinct No. 11, household no. 27.

12. See William Lynwood Montell, *Ghosts Along the Cumberland: Deathlore in the Kentucky Foothills* (Knoxville: University of Tennessee Press, 1975).

13. Ernest W. Baughman, *Type and Motif-Index of the Folktales of England and North America,* Indiana University Folklore Series, no. 20 (The Hague, The Netherlands: Mouton, 1966). Alternately, see Thompson, *Motif-Index of Folk Literature,* vol. 2, 428ff.

14. Maria Leach, ed., *Funk & Wagnall's Standard Dictionary of Folklore, Mythology and Legend* (New York: Harper & Row, 1984), 148.

15. Ibid.

Chapter 10. Restless Coffins

1. John Godwin, *This Baffling World* (New York: Hart Publishing, 1968), 215.

2. Rupert T. Gould, *Oddities* (1928; reprint, New Hyde Park, N.Y.: University Books, 1966), 23-51.

3. J. E. Alexander, *Transatlantic Sketches* (1933), in Gould, *Oddities,* 24.

4. Algernon E. Aspinall, *West Indian Tales of Old* (1915; reprint, New York: Negro Universities Press, 1969), 224.

5. Ibid., 225.

6. Gould, *Oddities,* 24.

7. Lucas/Orderson account, "The Lucas Manuscript Volumes," *Journal of the Barbados Museum and Historical Society* 12, no. 3 (May 1945): 57.

8. Ibid., 55, n. 12.

9. Alexander, *Transatlantic Sketches,* in Gould, *Oddities,* 24.

10. Robert H. Schomburgk, *History of Barbados* (London: Longman, Brown, Green and Longmans, 1848), 220-221.

11. Lucas/Orderson account, "Lucas Manuscript," 57.

12. Anonymous pamphlet, *Death-Deeds: An Extraordinary Incident Connected with Barbadoes* (London: Charles J. Skeet, 1860), 10.

13. Lucas/Orderson account, "Lucas Manuscript," 57.

14. Ibid., 56.

15. Gould, *Oddities,* 48.

16. Cf. Fig. 9 of Gould, *Oddities,* 32, with the sketch "From the manuscript of the Hon. Nathan Lucas," in Godwin, *Baffling World,* 221.

17. Lucas/Orderson account, "Lucas Manuscript," 57; Godwin, *Baffling World*, sketch on p. 221.

18. Gould, *Oddities*, 30.

19. Ibid., 24.

20. Ibid., 41.

21. Iris M. Owen, "The Moving Coffins of Barbados," *New Horizons*, April 1975; reprinted as "The Restless Coffins of Barbados," in *The World's Great Unsolved Mysteries*, ed. Martin Ebon (New York: Signet, 1981), 170–76.

22. Gould, *Oddities*, 46.

23. Godwin, *Baffling World*, 224.

24. Gould, *Oddities*, 42.

25. Ibid., 44–45.

26. Lucas/Orderson account, "Lucas Manuscript," 57.

27. Hugh Foster, Barbados Board of Tourism, letter to Joe Nickell, 22 November 1979.

28. Letters to Joe Nickell, 21 November 1979; 10 March 1980.

29. Algernon Aspinall, "An Unsolved Barbados Mystery," *Journal of the Barbados Museum and Historical Society* 13 (1945): 126.

30. Gould, *Oddities*, 23–24.

31. Aspinall, "Barbados Mystery," 126–127.

32. J. (sic) W. Orderson, *Creoleana, or Social and Domestic Scenes and Incidents in Barbados in Days of Yore* (London: Saunders and Otley, 1842), vi.

33. Joe Nickell, "Uncovered—The Fabulous Silver Mines of Swift and Filson," *Filson Club History Quarterly* 54, no. 4 (October 1980): 325–345.

34. Arthur Edward Waite, *A New Encyclopedia of Freemasonry*, vol. 1 (New York: Weathervane Books, 1970), 367.

35. Nickell, "Fabulous Silver Mines," 334.

36. Malcolm C. Duncan, *Duncan's Masonic Ritual and Monitor* (Chicago: Ezra A. Cook, 1972), 252.

37. Joe Nickell, "Discovered: The Secret of Beale's Treasure," *The Virginia Magazine of History and Biography* 90 (1982): 310–324.

38. *Revised Knight Templarism Illustrated* (Chicago: Ezra A. Cook, 1975), 64 n. 22.

39. Gertrude Jobes, *Dictionary of Mythology, Folklore and Symbols*, vol. 1 (New York: Scarecrow, 1961), 335.

40. Lucas/Orderson account, "Lucas Manuscript," 58.

41. Robert Macoy, *Illustrated History and Cyclopedia of Freemasonry* (New York: Macoy, 1908), 530.

42. Duncan, *Masonic Ritual and Monitor*, 242.

43. Macoy, *Cyclopedia of Freemasonry*, 671.

44. Lucas/Orderson account, "Lucas Manuscript," 57.

45. Macoy, *Cyclopedia of Freemasonry,* 234.

46. Ibid.; see also Duncan, *Masonic Ritual and Monitor,* 172.

47. Macoy, *Cyclopedia of Freemasonry,* 234; see also ibid., 454; cf. Lucas/ Orderson account, "Lucas Manuscript," 57.

48. Lucas/Orderson account, "Lucas Manuscript," 57.

49. Masonic Heirloom Edition Holy Bible. (Wichita, Kans.: Heirloom Bible Publishers, 1964), 24.

50. Macoy, *Cyclopedia of Freemasonry,* 472.

51. A. G. Mackey, *The Symbolism of Freemasonry* (Chicago: Powner, 1975), 349.

52. Duncan, *Masonic Ritual and Monitor,* 268.

53. Macoy, *Cyclopedia of Freemasonry,* 550.

54. Andrew Lang, " 'Death's Deeds': A Bi-Located Story," *Folk-Lore,* December 1907, 382ff.

55. Gould, *Oddities,* 27.

56. Macoy, *Cyclopedia of Freemasonry,* 83.

57. Godwin, *Baffling World,* 226.

58. A. Conan Doyle, "The Uncharted Coast," *Strand,* December 1919, 543–550.

59. Duncan, *Masonic Ritual and Monitor,* 124.

60. Harold V. B. Voorhis, "Sherlock Holmes Was a Mason," *Royal Arch Mason* 8 (Winter 1965): 248; Cecil A. Ryder, Jr., "A Study in Masonry," *The Sherlock Holmes Journal* 11, no. 3 (Winter 1973): 86–88.

61. A. Conan Doyle, "The Musgrave Ritual" and "The Adventure of Shoscome Old Place," in *The Complete Sherlock Holmes* (Garden City, N.Y.: Garden City Books, n.d.).

62. Lang, *"Death's Deeds,"* 379.

63. Robert Dale Owen, *Footfalls on the Boundary of Another World* (Philadelphia: Lippincott, 1869), 260–271.

64. Lang, "Death's Deeds," 378–379.

65. Owen, *Footfalls,* 266; cf. Waite, *New Encyclopedia of Freemasonry,* xx, and Macoy, *Cyclopedia of Freemasonry,* 676.

66. Owen, *Footfalls,* 263; cf. Duncan, *Masonic Ritual and Monitor,* 236.

67. Cecil O. Goodin, Arctic Lodge no. 394, F. & A M., undated note penned at bottom of Joe Nickell's letter of 19 January 1980.

68. "The Curious Vault at Stanton in Suffolk," *European Magazine,* September 1815.

69. Lucas/Orderson account, "Lucas Manuscript," 58.

70. Mrs. G. R. Hamilton, Christ Church, Barbados, letters to Joe Nickell, 23 February; 5 May 1981. She cites E. G. Sinckler, *Handbook of Barbados* (1913).

71. Mary, Viscountess Combermere, and Capt. W. W. Knollys, *Memoirs*

and Correspondence of Field-Marshal Viscount Combermere. . . . (London: Hurst and Blackett, 1866), 389.

72. Anonymous pamphlet, *Death-Deeds,* 10; Gould, *Oddities,* 25.

73. Viscountess Combermere, *Memoirs and Correspondence,* 392; Macoy, *Cyclopedia of Freemasonry,* 541 (cf. ibid., 593).

74. Viscountess Combermere, *Memoirs and Correspondence,* 392.

75. Macoy, *Cyclopedia of Freemasonry,* 231; Duncan, *Masonic Ritual and Monitor,* 228; Mackey, *Symbolism of Freemasonry,* 156.

76. Duncan, *Masonic Ritual and Monitor,* 244.

77. Ibid., 257.

78. Personal communications, 1980.

79. Mrs. G. R. Hamilton, letters to Joe Nickell, 23 February; 5 May 1981.

80. Aspinall, "Barbados Mystery," 130–131.

81. Macoy, *Cyclopedia of Freemasonry,* 323.

82. *Revised Knight Templarism Illustrated,* 242ff.

Chapter 11. Fiery Fate

1. W. S. Allen, "Weird Cremation," *True Detective,* December 1951, 42–45, 93–94.

2. "How Woman Was Incinerated Stumps All But Amateurs," *Atlanta Constitution,* 6 July 1951, 2.

3. Larry Arnold, "Human Fireballs," *Science Digest,* October 1981, 88–91, 115.

4. Vincent H. Gaddis, *Mysterious Fires and Lights* (New York: David McKay, 1967), 263.

5. Allan W. Eckert, "The Baffling Burning Death," *True,* May 1964, 33, 104.

6. Joe Nickell and John F. Fischer, "Spontaneous Human Combustion," *The Fire and Arson Investigator* 34, no. 3 (March 1984): 4–11; no. 4 (June 1984): 3–8.

7. George Henry Lewes, "Spontaneous Combustion," *Blackwood's Edinburgh Magazine* 89 (April 1861): 385–402.

8. Justus von Liebig, *Familiar Letters on Chemistry,* letter no. 22 (London: Taylor, Walton & Maberly, 1851).

9. See Appendix, case 1.

10. Ibid., case 2.

11. Ibid., case 3.

12. Ibid., case 4.

13. Ibid., case 5.

14. Ibid., case 8.

15. Ibid., case 12.

16. Ibid., case 18.

17. Ibid., case 20.

18. Lewes, "Spontaneous Combustion," 398.

19. D. J. Gee, "A Case of 'Spontaneous Combustion,'" *Medicine, Science and the Law* 5 (1965): 37–38.

20. Stevenson, *Medical Jurisprudence,* Appendix 2, case 13.

21. Liebig, *Familiar Letters,* letter no. 20.

22. Allen, "Weird Cremation," 94.

23. Werner U. Spitz and Russell S. Fischer, *Medicolegal Investigation of Death* (Springfield, Ill.: C. C. Thomas, 1980), 251.

24. D. J. X. Halliday, letter to editor, *New Scientist,* 29 May 1986.

25. Laurence D. Gadd and the editors of the World Almanac, *The Second Book of the Strange* (Buffalo, N.Y.: Prometheus Books, 1981), 35.

26. Ibid., 33–36.

27. Allen, "Weird Cremation," 45.

28. Gaddis, *Mysterious Fires and Lights,* 256.

29. Jerry Blizin, "The Reeser Case," *St. Petersburg Times* (Florida), 9 August 1951.

30. Thomas J. Ohlemiller, letters to Joe Nickell, 29 November 1982; 18 February 1983.

31. Allen, "Weird Cremation," 42ff.

32. Ibid., 45.

33. Wilton M. Krogman, "The Improbable Case of the Cinder Woman," *General Magazine and Historical Chronicle,* Winter 1953, 63.

34. David Wolf, interview by Joe Nickell, 15 May 1983.

35. Lemoyne Snyder, *Homicide Investigation,* 2nd ed. (Springfield, Ill.: C. C. Thomas, 1967), 233, 242.

Chapter 12. Afterword

1. Anyone may be deceived. But to be gulled *easily*—to be fooled when a reasonably cautious person would not be—is the meaning of the word *gullible*. See *Webster's New International Dictionary of the English Language,* 2nd ed., unabr. (Springfield, Mass.: G. & C. Merriam, 1955).

2. See chap. 6.

INDEX

Note: Italicized page numbers refer to illustrations.